FAITH ED.

TEACHING ABOUT RELIGION
IN AN AGE OF INTOLERANCE

LINDA K. WERTHEIMER

Beacon Press
Boston

Beacon Press
Boston, Massachusetts
www.beacon.org

Beacon Press books
are published under the auspices of
the Unitarian Universalist Association of Congregations.

19 18 17 16   8 7 6 5 4 3 2 1

This book is printed on acid-free paper that meets the uncoated paper
ANSI/NISO specifications for permanence as revised in 1992.

Text design by Ruth Maassen

Library of Congress Cataloging-in-Publication Data
Wertheimer, Linda.
Faith ed. : teaching about religion in an age of intolerance / Linda K. Wertheimer.
pages cm
Includes bibliographical references and index.
ISBN 978-0-8070-5527-4 (paperback : alk. paper) — ISBN 978-0-8070-8617-9 (ebook) 1.
Religion in the public schools—United States. 2. Education—Curricula—United States. I. Title.
LC111.W47 2015
379.2'80973—dc23
2014046389

*For my parents, who always made me believe
I could be a writer; for my husband, Pavlik,
who was there for me every step of this literary
journey; and for my son, Simon. May this
book make a difference for his generation.*

*In memory of Kevin Lee Wertheimer
(1962–1986), my fun-loving brother who lived
some of the stories in this book with me.*

I hold that it is the duty of every cultured man or woman to read sympathetically the scriptures of the world. If we are to respect others' religions as we would have them to respect our own, a friendly study of the world's religions is a sacred duty.

—Mahatma Gandhi (1869–1948),
from *All Religions Are True*

CONTENTS

PROLOGUE

I sat in the safest place I knew, stunned by what I was hearing:
   A swastika and the words "Jews Kill Them All" etched on a
      playground slide.
   Swastikas painted on the boy's bathroom at the high school.
   A pair of first-grade boys playing a game they called Jail the Jews.

THESE INCIDENTS all happened at schools in Bedford, the suburban Boston town next door to mine. In March 2014, I sat among nearly two hundred people in my temple sanctuary as rabbis, parents, and the superintendent of Bedford schools described what had happened. My temple and the town I have lived in for a decade are the safest havens I've known as a Jew. But on that night, I no longer felt so at ease as a Jew in my town. I wasn't afraid for myself but I feared that my son's innocence could be shattered if the anti-Semitism spread.

What shook me most were the ages of the children who played a game with an anti-Semitic undertone. They were just six or seven, a year older than my son at the time. How could any child think it was okay to play a game called Jail the Jews? It was, in fact, a Christian boy's parents who had alerted the school system to the game. The parents were mortified. Where did such young children come up with such a name for a game? They must have heard that language from adults. I did not believe children that young created the game out of hate. They created it out of ignorance.

Hearing about the game and the swastikas painted on school walls and etched on playground equipment stirred painful memories. When I was nine, my family moved to a rural Ohio town where my brothers and I were the only Jewish children in our school and where there were no temples. We were the target of anti-Semitic remarks but never complained. We figured it would further single us out as different. As an adult, I chose to live in a town with many Jews and several synagogues because I did not want to relive the experiences of my childhood. When I became a mother, I wanted to shield my son from the hurt I'd once felt. He should never feel ashamed or scared to identify himself as a Jew, as I had been for years.

Many people lined up to speak as meeting organizers sought comments at the forum at my temple. Their willingness to tell their stories helped me move from desolation to optimism. There was little anger that night. Instead, there was talk of hope. A group of town clergy was creating a campaign called Love Your Neighbor to bring different religious groups together. Bedford High School decided to introduce a curriculum about the history of anti-Semitism and of hate toward other minority groups, and the school system started examining more ways to teach elementary students how to respect differences. There hadn't been just one incident at the town's two elementary schools, the superintendent told us. Jewish students, while the target in most cases, also eagerly participated in a game of tag called Jews versus Christians. A Christian child threatened to destroy a classmate's country because the girl was Jewish. In a conversation about Hanukkah, Christian children accused Jews of killing Jesus Christ.[1]

That night at my temple, memories of the past led me to walk from my seat in the second row to the front of the sanctuary. I stood at the microphone on the carpeted floor below the bimah, where the rabbis give sermons. "These things will stay with you forever," I said, my voice cracking as I referred to remarks I'd heard throughout childhood. Others who spoke proposed fixes, though none of them quick ones. A Christian woman who married a Jew and was raising her children Jewish talked about the need for schools to teach children that they have the power to say something to fellow students who malign another group. A sophomore at Bedford High School remembered how peers in middle school threw pennies at her as a jab at the stereotype about Jews and money. But she did not think the principal's recent talk to students about anti-Semitism had made a difference. Many teens shrugged his words off. Rather, this teen wanted to see her school attempt to teach students about many religions instead of focusing on one. The students at her temple's religious school toured other houses of worship and talked with people of different faiths, including Buddhism and Christianity. She and her Jewish peers realized how little they had known about other faiths and had shed some of their misconceptions.

The teen's idea could not have been better, given how the debate about religion's place in the schools has shifted. No longer are we arguing about whether teachers can lead students in the Lord's Prayer and recite Bible verses. The Supreme Court settled that about fifty years ago by ruling that it was wrong for schools to promote one religion over another. Today, many schools are sorting out the best ways to reduce ignorance about religion. Religion became a dividing line for some children in Bedford, a scenario that can and does happen in schools across America. Religious minorities have faced much worse than graffiti and prejudicial remarks, both inside and outside classrooms. Children have yanked off the turbans of young Sikhs as they waited to board a school bus, and they have taunted Muslim peers on anniversaries of the 9/11 attacks. Sikhs, Muslims, and Hindus live in my community and in nearby towns. So do atheists. All of those groups can easily be targets because their beliefs are rarely understood. Can education soften the divisions? What can schools do and what are they already doing to ensure the next generation will not need to hold forums to confront religious intolerance?

CHAPTER ONE

Burkagate

SHARON PETERS reached into a hot-pink cloth bag and pulled out an *abaya*, a full-length body garment for women, from Kuwait. As if she were modeling for a fashion show, the world geography teacher stuck her arms out sideways and held the garment against her to show how far it stretched, from the tips of the fingers on one hand to those on the other. She slipped her arms through, letting the black polyester cloth hang loosely from her shoulders to her moccasin-clad feet. She apologized for her inauthenticity; normally she would wear sandals. Next, she held a black, filmy veil to her face, then repeated what she always said to her freshman advanced geography students in Lumberton, a dot of a town one hundred miles east of Houston, near the Louisiana border. "I want you to put it in front of your face so you can see how others in the world live," she said. Imagine, she added in her native southeast Texas twang, what it would be like to see the world through gauze.

Like a magician about to unveil the next trick, she reached into the bag again and clutched a royal-blue burka from Afghanistan, a garment that conceals the wearer from head to toe and includes mesh over the eyes. This was the item, she said, that caused "our

1

famous burka incident." Her previously gentle tone turned stern: "This is the only damn burka."[1]

It was the fall of September 2013 and Peters was giving me an impromptu fashion show in the living room of her one-story ranch home in Lumberton. She didn't try on the burka because it was child-sized, okay for a very short teen but not for an adult who was about five feet, six inches tall. She relived the day she'd given her customary lesson, which for nearly fifteen years had been part of her instruction about Islam and the Middle East. During her February 1, 2013, class, as always, students took photos of one another. But this time a student posted a photo on Facebook of four girls and one boy wearing the outfits, including the burka. The picture went viral, causing an uproar that some teachers dubbed "burka-gate." For several weeks it was as if Peters's entire thirty-nine-year teaching career was under attack. Strangers sent e-mails accusing her and the school system of corrupting children and attempting to convert them to Islam. Already sixty-three, Peters had been thinking of retiring at the end of that school year. The controversy sealed the decision.

To understand the ire that Peters and the Lumberton school system faced, it helps to know something about Lumberton and about the state of Texas and its messy relationship with religion and the public schools. A town of roughly twelve thousand, Lumberton sits a ways off of Interstate 10 in an area that's called the Big Thicket because of its abundance of tall pines. Lumberton's beginnings date to the late 1800s and an area called Hook's Switch. The town's name stems from its origins as a lumber town with a sawmill along the Southern Pacific Railroad.[2] But Lumberton did not incorporate until 1973. Nearby Beaumont began integrating its schools and an increasing number of white people started leaving for Lumberton, determined not to send their children to school with black children. Many Lumberton residents openly call their community a "white flight" town and say the Ku Klux Klan used to be fairly active. "Why do you think I moved here?" a father of a Lumberton

High student told me as we chatted in his home about the burka to-do. "I didn't want to live near blacks."[3] The town has improved in racial relations: used to be, black drivers in the region would be afraid to stop at a store in Lumberton because of the town's racist reputation.[4] Even today, less than 1 percent of Lumberton's population is black and barely 5 percent is Hispanic; the rest is white.[5] It's hard to drive even a tenth of a mile without seeing a church in this largely working-class community, where many residents work for the nearby oil refineries. Less than a quarter of the residents have a bachelor's degree or higher and just 4 percent have a graduate degree. The mean family income is roughly $65,000.[6] The predominant religion is Baptist. Most churches are either Protestant or Methodist, save for a lone Catholic parish.

Lumberton, a mix of trailer parks, new home developments, and country living, boasts a mobile-home sales business on its Main Street, a few yards from an outfitter that provides canoes for a paddle at Village Creek State Park. Teachers say the percentage of impoverished students is rising, and state data back that up. A third of Lumberton's students qualify for free- or reduced-price lunches.[7] My choices for lodging were limited to low-budget hotels or a year-old bed-and-breakfast, which billed itself as a great place for writers. I chose the B&B, called the Book Nook Inn, but questioned my choice as I drove in pelting rain down a rural road alongside the Big Thicket Preserve and the Pine Island Bayou. There was scant sign of civilization, save for a mobile home here and there. I almost drove past the inn, a white, Victorian-style house with a widow's walk set at the end of a gravel driveway, which the rain had transformed into a mud slick. I had come at the start of fall during hurricane season and in the thick of lovebug season. One of the little black-winged insects fell into my shirt as I entered my lodging, a pool cabin across from the inn. Lovebugs ended up on the cabin floor, in the shower, on my rental car windows, and on me throughout my time in Lumberton. These pests became part of my rather surreal experience in the town, where it was not always easy to be a stranger asking about a controversy many residents wanted to forget. For some towns-people and school officials, it was embarrassing to have gained no-toriety because local high school students had tried on burkas and abayas as part of a lesson on Islam. The news coverage made it seem as if Lumberton was liberal and progressive but the town's residents preferred to depict themselves as ultraconservative. The school has a strict dress code to match the conservative flavor. Boys' hair can-not touch their collars, hang over their eyes, or drift over their ears. Tattoos must be covered.[8]

Town and school officials in Lumberton saw it as a Christian town where it was acceptable and encouraged to show a love for Jesus in the public arena. At city council meetings, members prayed at the beginning to thank the good lord for what they had, Mayor Don Surratt said as we chatted in his office in the one-story town office building catty-corner to a Dairy Queen on Main Street. Surratt, a Baptist, has lived in Lumberton since 1964 and has been the town's mayor for eleven years. The seventy-four-year-old grandfather of three said frankly that he preferred Lumberton schools to focus on teaching students about Christianity and America. He saw no need for students to put on clothing from other countries. "Why should you teach about other religions and not the one you're in?" he said, leaning back in his leather chair as the eyes of two bucks' heads stared at me from just above him. Five hunting trophies, including an Afri-can antelope he'd shot on a Texas hunting preserve, were the office's main decor. He gave a soliloquy regarding his concerns about this country. "They come over here and they don't work. If they don't do it legally, they should move back. That's my opinion," he said, draw-ing out the word "my." "Who are you talking about, 'they'?" I asked.

"I don't like to point out different ethnic groups. You've been around this country. You know what's happening to it."

I refrained from comment because if I'd said what I felt, the conversation would have ended there.

If the school was going to teach about Islam and how Muslims have to wear burkas, then it should also teach about Christianity and why Jesus died on the cross, he said. Students, he believed, could learn about other religions outside of school, on television, in the newspapers. They did not need a class. "What I know about Muslims is how they treat you or your sex. We have a few people who went to Saudi Arabia. Women can't drive," he attested.

But what, I asked, about American Muslims? "I know a couple of them," he said. "If they want to come over here, they need to speak our language." He was quick to say that he didn't fear Muslims. "But I'm always watching. I'm always alert."

Surratt said his biggest concern was seeing so many attempts to diminish Christianity. The Freedom from Religion Foundation, a Wisconsin group, had protested that summer after a Lumberton principal led graduating kindergartners in a prayer in Jesus's name. Worse, outsiders had complained about the Bible verse the police department keeps on the front page of its website. "We have several people call from Michigan, another state, people from Dallas. It's people who don't believe in Christ, atheists, people like that," he said.

"They might be Jews, Hindus, Muslims," I said.

"I think they're atheists," he said.

At the mayor's suggestion, I walked across the city hall parking lot to get a deeper Lumberton history lesson from David Lisenby, the executive director of the town's chamber of commerce. Lisenby, also a parent of a Lumberton student, had a much different outlook from the mayor. Lisenby's daughter, a senior in the fall of 2013, had taken Peters's class a few years before. Lisenby saw nothing wrong with either the burka exercise or the goal to teach about other religions and countries. It was a great concept, he said, to use clothes as a teaching tool. "How can you experience the seventies without putting on those tight bell bottoms?" the fifty-one-year-old said as he stood in his paper-strewn office, talking and simultaneously looking for a pamphlet on Lumberton's history. "Women in Saudi Arabia, in the Islamic community, have to cover their face. Can you imagine what those women have to go through over there? No, not till you put on those layers of clothing, and you have that thing over your face and your eyes, and you're breathing." And, he added, it was hot in that part of the world, as hot as southeast Texas could get in the summer. The day we talked it was 90 degrees. His hope was that his daughter's generation would develop a mindset different from people of his generation and older in southeast Texas. If they were more exposed to diversity, more exposed to tolerance and acceptance, maybe they would, in turn, be more tolerant and accepting.

The area's passion for Christianity really came into focus for me when David Hearne, the B&B's co-owner, invited me to a release party for his latest self-published book, *The Christmas Special*. The novel chronicles a series of Muslim terrorist attacks on Christmas morning, and central characters include an Afghani doctor who's really an Islamic terrorist. Hearne's wife, Stacie, decorated the living room and dining area in honor of the book, putting up a Christmas tree and lights. Even the dessert—red velvet cupcakes—matched the theme. In person, David Hearne, a New Hampshire native, did not come across as particularly fearful of Muslims and seemed moderate politically. He adhered to no particular religion, while his wife, born in a nearby Texas town, described herself as a Southern Baptist.

At the party, two guests told me how hard it was to be atheist or agnostic in a region where people began meetings with prayers and Wednesdays were set aside for church youth group meetings. That tradition was so embedded that schools knew better than to schedule events on Wednesday nights. Another guest talked nonstop to me for nearly a half hour about the still-brewing controversy in the nearby town of Kountze, where cheerleaders held banners displaying Bible verses each week at the high school football game. Kountze mirrors Lumberton in religious demographics but racially is more diverse; about 25 percent of its 2,100 residents are black.[9] The cheerleaders had made numerous religious banners, including ones that pronounced, "I can do all things through Christ which strengthens me" and "But thanks be to God which gives us victory through our Lord Jesus Christ."[10] The school district, citing separation of church and state, tried to stop the practice in 2012. The cheerleaders sued and, in the spring of 2013, a lower court ruled in their favor.

At a football game I attended in Kountze, cheerleaders unraveled a banner that read, "And he said, 'The things which are impossible with men are possible with God,'" from Luke 18:27. Cheerleaders, some sitting on one another's shoulders, held the banner as the Kountze football team ran through and broke the paper in half. The crowd cheered. A short while later an announcer asked everyone to stand for a moment of silence. Everyone around me bowed their heads while I stood with my head up, watching as I had done throughout high school in rural Ohio when pastors came to my school and led us in prayer. "Amen," someone shouted to end the moment of silence, and people applauded. Lumberton has no banners with Bible verses at its football games but lets a student group lead the crowd in prayer. No one has protested and school officials say the practice merely reflects the community's values.

Court rulings on prayer at football games have been tough to sort out. The US Supreme Court in 2000 ruled against allowing student-led prayers over district-owned public address systems in a case involving another small Texas high school, Santa Fe.[11] A year later, the court refused to hear an appeal of a lower court's ruling that allowed student-led prayers at Alabama football games.[12] I repeatedly heard this refrain from Lumberton residents: if no one was complaining, what was the big deal, given that we lived in a Christian nation? There was an irony about the Kountze dispute: in 1991 Kountze elected the country's first Muslim mayor, a signal to many that the town embraced religious differences. But that election was a decade before Muslim terrorists struck the World Trade Center towers.

Guests at the book party had mixed views on Kountze's banners. The cheerleaders had a right to their freedom of religious expression, some said. Why not let the cheerleaders hold up those Bible verses, and if others disliked them, they could make their own banners? Those in opposition said the banners imposed one belief on everyone and were the equivalent of a government body promoting Christianity because cheerleaders represented the school. Supporters of the cheerleaders seemed to be winning the popular vote: a Facebook page, "Heading On: Support Kountze Kids Faith," attracted more than 42,000 followers—about 20 times the population of Kountze. Opponents I met, though, said they felt a little paranoid about the idea of going public with views that others perceived as ungodly. No one wanted to become the talk of the town. There was even paranoia about my coming to Lumberton. During my visit to his office, the chamber of commerce's executive director told me with a bemused smile that my presence in Lumberton had been noted in the town's Facebook circles and that the word was to not talk to me. The schools superintendent had even received a phone call from a parent urging him not to speak to me. "We are a cartoon of a small town," one resident told me as we talked over tea in a Beaumont café a mile from Lumberton. She had met with me to show her support for Peters's class and for how it had helped broaden her daughter's point of view.[13]

It was not just the mores of a small town that Peters was testing when she incorporated lessons about world religion into her geography classes. She was messing with the mores of vocal ultraconservatives throughout Texas. Texas, like most states, requires students to learn about religions as part of world geography and world history courses, a state standard since 1998. But, joining only a handful of states, it also passed a law in 2008 requiring all high schools to offer electives about the Bible in literature or history if there was enough student interest. Several school systems offer the courses, and several classes have been criticized for serving more as vehicles for proselytizing than for academic study of the Bible.[14] The Texas State Board of Education, meanwhile, has tussled repeatedly over content in science and history textbooks and over how or whether religion should play a role. For nearly two decades Texas required biology teachers and textbooks to include strengths and weaknesses of Charles Darwin's theory of evolution, keeping the door open for teachers to include lessons about creationism.[15] The board dropped that requirement in 2009.

A year later, some state board members complained that some of the state's adopted history books had a pro-Islamic bias. They proposed a resolution telling publishers not to "present a pro-Islamic, anti-Christian version of history if you want to sell books in one of the nation's largest markets." The resolution went so far as to say that the textbooks gave more space to Islam than to Christianity and were kinder to Islam than to Christianity in their depictions.[16] The measure passed, 7–6, leading one of the resolution's opponents to say, "This makes us look cuckoo."[17] Tired of the board's shenanigans, the state legislature in 2012 took away its control over textbooks in Texas public schools. Previously, schools could not get state funds for books unless the board had approved them. Now, schools can pick books that are not on the approved list. In 2013, though, board members were back at it again, squabbling over whether to adopt a textbook because one reviewer, a staunch supporter of creationism, said a particular textbook presented faulty arguments on evolution. The board ultimately approved the book.

Peters, who converted from Catholicism to Judaism in 2002, was born and raised in Port Arthur, a nearby town along the Gulf Coast. She knew she was playing with a little fire every time she talked about religion. Long before the burka controversy, a parent had protested an assignment that required students to do a project about a Hindu god. A parent told Peters that her child would not do the assignment unless the student was allowed to use a Christian personality. Though she was furious, Peters granted the request. But when another parent opposed Peters teaching about religion as part of geography, the teacher did not back down. "I was emphatic. This is part of culture. This is who you are. This is how you think, how you act because of your religion," Peters said, sitting in a plush gray chair in front of her bookcase, which included books about Daoism, Judaism, Christianity, and other faiths. When teaching about a region or country, she spoke about the religion of the area as it came up. Christianity was included in discussions of Europe. When students studied India, they learned about Hindus, Sikhs, and Muslims and a little about the Jews who lived there. North and South America brought discussion about several religions, including Catholicism. When the students moved on to East Asia, they learned about Daoism, Shintoism, and Buddhism. Peters was a woman on a mission, determined to show her students a world beyond rural southeast Texas. She liked to tell them, "Wake up. You don't live behind the Pine Curtain."

News reports quoted school district officials saying Peters collected the Muslim clothing on world travels. That was incorrect. The travels of the divorced mother of three were minimal. A mini sculpture of the Eiffel Tower on her bookcase was a souvenir from one of her few forays abroad. She had never been to the Middle East. The burka that caused the stir was a gift from a student's father, who bought it while he was on a business trip in Afghanistan. After showing me the abaya and the burka, Peters reached a slender hand into her bag again and pulled out a pile of white cotton clothing, all for males in Saudi Arabia. Men, she told students, got to wear cotton, a lighter, more breathable material, while women often had to wear a heavier material, making them all the more uncomfortable in the heat of the Middle East. A former home economics teacher who also taught fashion design at Lumberton High, she sewed most of the male clothing herself. Her collection included a *thawb*, a long-sleeved, ankle-length white garment, and a *ghutra*, a scarf-like headdress, which her brother gave her after traveling to Saudi Arabia. She ended her demonstration for me by holding up a kaftan, an overcoat that men put over a *thawb*. In the classroom, she put most of the clothing on a table and let students pick what they wanted to try on, the same activity she did with other countries' apparel.

"Can you see?" she asked students who tried on the burka or veils. "Walk around. How does that feel?" They answered, she recalled, that they could not see much or they commented on how hot and stifling it was to wear the clothing. That same day she taught another lesson that became fodder for debate. She gave students a handout titled "Case Studies: Revolutionaries or Terrorists," part of an online exercise for students provided by the PBS program *NewsHour*. The students were asked to examine several case studies and decide if a case represented terrorism or another form of political violence. The examples included incidents from Northern Ireland, Chechnya, Mexico, South Africa, and the United States.[18] She used the lesson to spark discussion and asked students to analyze each situation in writing and decide if the agitators were freedom fighters or terrorists. She wanted them to realize that the way one person perceived something might be different from the way someone else did.

As her students snapped photos, she never thought about Facebook and what might happen if they posted the photos there. Students from six classes tried on the clothes the same day. In the photo that became infamous, there were five teens: a girl in the blue burka, a girl in a *hijab* (the traditional head covering that Muslim females wear), a boy in the Saudi Arabian *thawb* and a kaffiyeh (a headdress made of a square cloth), and two students each in a chador (a full-body garment women wrap around their heads as well as their bodies in Iran). They stood in front of the classroom whiteboard, on which Peters had printed headings for Islam, Judaism, and Christianity and the religions' branches or divisions. Parents of two students became incensed when they saw the photo of their daughters in the Muslim garments. What happened next blindsided the veteran teacher.

The first story broke on a conservative blog, *WorldNetDaily*, on February 24, 2013. Headlined "Students Made to Wear Burqas—in Texas," the story linked the burka lesson to a Texas online curriculum that conservatives had attacked for allegedly having a pro-Islam bias. But Peters's lessons predated the creation of that curriculum, which provides lesson plans to teachers. *WorldNetDaily*, quoting unnamed students, contended Peters told her students that she was supposed to teach them to refer to Muslims as freedom fighters rather than terrorists.[19] The next day a Lumberton-based blogger and Lumberton High graduate, David Bellow, repeated the story on his blog and added his own commentary. He refuted some of *WorldNetDaily*'s contentions, saying no one had been forced to wear a burka, but he called the freedom fighter lesson "outrageous." The story went national when a student of Peters, Madelyn McLemore, and her mother, April LeBlanc, were featured in a Fox News Radio report and then on a Fox-TV story titled "Education or Indoctrination? TX Public School Kids Don Islamic Garb." In the radio report, Lumberton schools superintendent John Valastro defended Peters, whose name was not given to the media. Valastro told Fox News that the teacher had done nothing wrong. "What is more dangerous: fear and ignorance, or education and understanding?" he said. "From our standpoint, we are here to educate the kids." Valastro told Fox he did not believe the teacher was downplaying radical Islam. The mother and her daughter, then fifteen, disagreed.

LeBlanc, the mother, told Fox that her biggest issue was not the burka. "That was the key to opening up the rest," she said in the Fox interview. "It's scary how far they dove into the Islamic faith. It's scary what they taught my daughter. Who's in charge of this? How did our superintendent let this slip through the cracks?" She was particularly upset about the lesson about freedom fighters versus terrorists: "This teacher taught her that a freedom fighter is when they give their life for the Holy War and that they're going to heaven. They were saturating these kids in Islam and my daughter is an American Christian child." Madelyn, who was in the Facebook photo, told Fox News that she felt terrible sitting through the lesson that tried to compare 9/11 hijackers to freedom fighters. Valastro countered that the teacher was merely trying to get students to think for themselves. The superintendent's response did not placate LeBlanc, who told Fox, "We trusted these people. It scares me. I feel like our school is being infiltrated. How can this not be a sign? We're talking about Lumberton, Texas. We're talking about a small town with Christian churches on every street corner. Right in our small school this is going on."[20]

School officials, hoping to quell a growing outrage, released a statement on February 25, a day after the first story came out, and said the lesson simply informed students about the culture of the people in the Middle East. The statement noted that the Facebook photo focused only on Middle Eastern attire, while the course covered several religions and cultures. The school district addressed the freedom fighter/terrorist lesson, saying the teacher used a quote from a book by Gerald Seymour: "One man's terrorist is another's freedom fighter." Peters later told me that she didn't use that quote; she just used the material from the *NewsHour* lessons. In its statement, Lumberton also tried to pacify those worried about a lack of attention to Christianity. It mentioned the Christian Bible study class available to all students, a reference to courses offered in the past on Bible literature. It also noted that the high school had several Christian groups, including Raiders for Christ, God's Team, and Kids for Christ. "The school district supports the viewpoints of Christian belief and welcomes students in the expression of their faith. The community of Lumberton is strongly dedicated to Christian beliefs and the faith is welcomed in our schools," the district statement concluded.[21] Lumberton school officials battled twin desires: to reassure the community that no one was shoving Christian values aside and to educate its students about a world far larger and diverse than the tiny Texas town.

The school system's statement did not seem to appease many. The *Beaumont Enterprise* published an editorial asking the school district to clarify what had happened because it was hard to determine the facts: "It appears to be a lesson about foreign cultures that may have been misinterpreted . . . or was badly conceived from the start."[22] Bellow, the local blogger, kept outrage going, some residents said, by writing so many posts about the burka controversy. Meeting with me at a McDonald's restaurant in Lumberton, Bellow said he didn't like what he heard about the freedom fighters and he didn't like the idea of kids trying on burkas. To the twenty-nine-year-old federal prison guard and aspiring politician, the reason for not trying on the burka was common sense. Putting on the item, in his view, was as inappropriate as trying on a priest's robe and practicing blessing someone with holy water. He knew students weren't forced to try on anything, but that did not matter because he thought they never should have been asked. What really vexed him was his sense that schools weren't allowed to teach much about Christianity anymore, and here was a teacher trying to glorify Islam. The country, he contended, was bending over backward to accommodate Muslims' desires to pray and express their beliefs while shunning Christianity. The fact that many Americans mocked then NFL quarterback Tim Tebow for praying before and during games proved his point. So did the fact that Kountze cheerleaders had to fight to keep their banners.

As he spoke, Bellow, unshaven with dark circles rimming his eyes, apologized for looking bedraggled, which was due to having stayed up with his ten-month-old baby the previous night. He was careful to emphasize that he was not one of those wackos with extreme anti-Muslim views. "I don't have any issue with Islam being in America and even with people learning in class in a balanced way about the different religions. I have no problem with it," he said. "Uh, I go to Happy Donuts on a regular basis. I have no problem with them having their Buddhist statue there." He paused, then pointed across the street at the shop in question as proof that Lumberton residents were not closed to other cultures and religions. After all, he said, "you don't see anybody suing Happy Donuts because they have a Buddha." That remark left me at a loss for words. A doughnut shop is not a public school classroom. It can stick voodoo dolls on a shelf if it wants to.

—〽—

After the Fox News reports came out, school officials received more than six hundred e-mails, most from out-of-towners. Some were threatening. Some were vile. "I cannot believe our schools that are supposed to keep religeon [*sic*] separate are having students dress in Muslim garb. That is beyond outrageous!!! This is Texas for God's sake!!! . . . You need to be teaching US and Texas history. . . . This is appaulling [*sic*] to read about," one person wrote. "According to Mr. Valastro's Left Wing reasoning, Adolf Hitler was just a hope and change politician, and the Mexican Drug Cartels are just Big Business. He is trying to indoctrinate the children with the left wing agenda. He should be fired," wrote another. "THIS IS NOT GEOGRAPHY. STOP LYING TO YOUR PARENTS!" another correspondent wrote. "Promotion of the Muslim religion, reading of the Koran, indoctrination of our children, teaching that Allah is God . . . where does this end???"[23]

Some people preferred to call, and Superintendent Valastro fielded some calls himself. "I was cussed out from Maryland to Washington State to Kansas to Afghanistan," the fifty-year-old schools chief told me as he sat behind the same desk where he answered those calls. He seemed more bemused than annoyed as he recalled the fuss. In each call, he tried to explain what the teacher was doing and that the controversy was over a misunderstanding. "Most of them understood we weren't being perverse. We weren't trying to glorify Islam or the Muslims. We were just teaching a lesson. You teach about Europe. You teach about Asia," he said in a matter-of-fact tone with a touch of Texas twang. He was born in Galveston and first made his name as a high school football coach. One of his teams won a state championship.[24] He was used to weathering criticism. It was a toss-up as to which was worse, the difficulty he experienced as a coach or as a superintendent during burkagate.

The school system shielded Peters from most of the e-mails, though she received a few hateful notes from people who easily figured out her identity. She was the only advanced geography teacher listed on the high school website. "Tar and feathering should be brought back, you fool," someone wrote Peters. "You go live in Saudi Arabia and have fun being beaten and having ZERO rights and being at fault for everything. Did you teach them that? You fool."[25] Shaken by the hate, she became paranoid about what she could say for a while and refused to talk about the class even when friends called. She put off watching the Fox News reports, and when she finally saw them, she was devastated. To her, the criticisms of her class were a personal vendetta against her teaching. Peters portrayed a mix of confidence and vulnerability when she spoke with me in her living room. Despite her midlength white hair, she looked younger than her years, with her dangling earrings and dancer's posture. Confidence came through in her voice and bearing when she described what she taught and why. Vulnerability poked through when she spoke of finding out that her lesson had made national news and that people were castigating her. Two students, including the one who spoke to Fox News, dropped her class. It became difficult to go to work and to hold back tears. At the high school, colleagues hugged her and students showered her with cards, flowers, and candy.[26]

She left the living room and brought back two pink posters covered with students' notes of admiration: "Everyone loves you and I think it's just pitiful that parents are being so naive. I hope they realize how idiotic they are being." . . . "Ms. Peters, I loved your class last year! I learned so much, and it opened my eyes up to the different cultures of the world!" . . . "Mrs. Peters, never let some unenlightened redneck channel tell you how to do your job. Hold fast to your convictions. Even if no one else will, I thank you for teaching that there is more than one opinion in the world."[27]

To some parents and students, she was a teacher with a hippie soul and a penchant for teaching about so many things foreign. To others, she was a bit kooky. Peters seemed more eclectic than kooky during the hours I spent with her. She beamed when she talked about her love for Daoism and the Dalai Lama. She insisted on providing lunch and arranged a buffet of Mediterranean food on her kitchen counter: stuffed grape leaves, hummus, baba ghanoush, couscous, yogurt dressing, and pita. As I was leaving she stuck a gift bag in my arms. "It's a Texas welcome," she said as I peeked inside at Texas jellies, honey, Peach-a-Rita mix, and a book, *Women Who Run With the Wolves*, which billed itself as a story about what's inside of every woman: a "wild, natural creature, filled with good instincts, passionate creativity and ageless knowing."[28] I couldn't help but wonder whether she gave me the book to remind me of her. She was a free spirit.

As public ire mounted, the Lumberton school board scheduled a meeting to address the controversy. Unsure of just how unpleasant the meeting could get, Peters stayed home. On March 7, 2013, roughly one hundred people filled the school board's meeting room, a full house for the modest-sized space and a school district of just 3,900 students. The meeting began in the normal way, with the Pledge of Allegiance followed by an invocation, this time by the school board attorney: "Heavenly father, we thank you, Lord, for the many blessings you give us every day. Father, we come to you tonight asking for your help . . . Father, give them your wisdom, Lord, and father, we ask, Lord, that this meeting might be conducted in peace and harmony. We ask all of these things in Jesus's name. Amen." "Amen," the crowd and board echoed.[29] The atmosphere started out as hostile when the first of eleven speakers began a diatribe against Muslims. That first speaker, a resident of Port Neches, a town about thirty miles south of Lumberton, contended that Muslims would think most everyone in the board room was an infidel because they did not practice Islam. He finished to scattered applause.

Another speaker, a man from neighboring Kountze, immediately won applause by noting that he had turned ninety the previous week. He made a point of telling everyone that he wore a World War II veterans' vest to keep the memory of veterans alive and that he'd woken up at two that morning to compose his speech because he was so upset by the goings on at Lumberton High. He used a special computer program to help him because he's legally blind. His caregiver, he announced, would now read his speech. What followed began as a history lesson, about how he remembered the 1930s, when there was no Lumberton. People fled Beaumont to the new town that would become Lumberton, a sanctuary from integration. The speaker went on:

> Today, we have this thriving city of Lumberton, Texas, all safe and secure from that tidal wave. But things change. You, like all American cities, are being silently invaded by others who may appear to be like you, but they are wolves in sheep's clothing. They are already here. Just like every big city in the United States, all of our small convenience stores and third-rate hotels are now owned and run by them. I am speaking of the nation of Islam, or Muslims.
>
> Now, you teachers have opened your schools to teach them by teaching that to dress like a Muslim female is honorable and praiseworthy, yet you are forbidden to teach these children about Jesus Christ or God because of the protests of a few atheists who don't believe in anything. It is called separation of church and state.

The speech also referenced the Kountze cheerleaders. The speaker saw it as an irony that the cheerleaders had to fight to use Christian verses at football games "while little Lumberton wants to teach these young children how nice it is to dress like the ladies of Islam in their cute burkas. Why? Those Islamic women you are teaching about have absolutely no rights at school. . . . We still have American men and women being killed by people who wear those styles of dress. Never forget, their Islam purpose in life is to kill infidels, and that includes everyone who is not Islam. And they hate Americans, like you and me. . . . How long will it be until little safe Lumberton, Texas, wakes up and finds a Muslim mosque in their safe little town? I ask you to please be very careful of what you program or teach into these little computer brains of these children today." As his speech ended, the audience responded with loud, raucous applause. Was it an endorsement of his views or a bow to the man's age and military service? The speech was chilling. In decades past, would a speaker have substituted Jews for Muslims?

The next two speakers pleaded for openness, education, and respect. Christy Skinner, an English teacher at Lumberton High, spoke as a teacher and a mother of twin seventeen-year-old daughters at the high school. Skinner, who had taught for seven years at Lumberton and for sixteen years elsewhere, knew Peters and liked her. More important, she knew Peters was just trying to do her job. Skinner realized that it could have been her on the hot seat. She could not imagine teaching Nathaniel Hawthorne's *The Scarlet Letter* without teaching about religion and about the Puritan beliefs regarding original sin. She beseeched parents to keep an open mind. "A parent's job is to teach children in the way that they should grow. However, a teacher's job, as Socrates said, is to help children develop an educated mind that can entertain a thought without accepting it. In our classrooms, we often challenge existing norms, and we often require students to consider events like 9/11 from the perspective of the aggressors and the victims."

Parents spoke for and against what had happened in the geography class. A supporter of Peters said the teacher was simply doing what was needed and people were overreacting because learning about Islam took many out of their comfort zone. An opponent of the lesson urged teachers to work with parents to rid schools of growing liberal-progressive influences. "Amen," an audience member said as huge applause followed. One woman, whose daughter wore the burka in the Facebook photo, told the crowd she was unsure where to start because she had so many issues after seeing her daughter in that clothing on the Internet. "Religion is very personal, very sensitive," she said. "I didn't want someone to be retaliated against by someone thinking these kids were being disrespectful to this attire." She questioned why the state was mixing religion with the schools and objected to the school asking her daughter and another student to fill out incident reports and sign statements without parents being present. Her daughter's peers had bullied her because of the photo. "My daughter didn't ask for this. She was in class. She was taking part in the event, wearing the clothes, yet she's had to pay a big price," the mother said.

Zachary Kellas, then a sophomore at Lumberton High, was the lone student speaker. He was his class president, a football player, and a member of the school's debate team. He had taken the same class his freshman year, tried on a *thawb* and other Saudi Arabian clothes for males, and posed for a photo. He still stored the photo on his cell phone. "It was fun. It was, 'Hey, I've never actually seen one of these in person. This is what a burka looks like.' The teacher said, 'If you'd like to try it on, you can, but you do not have to,'" he said in an even-keeled tone. As if he were the audience's teacher instead of the innocent child so many were trying to protect, he told them how studying different religions, including Islam and Buddhism, related to studying other countries. It was common sense. How could students learn about certain countries without hearing about the religious influences? Referring to a few speakers' concerns, he said he also held conservative political views and was not a victim of indoctrination by liberal progressives. He, like other teens at Lumberton High, was mature enough to develop his own views, he told the audience.

Valastro, who was finishing his second year as superintendent after more than a decade as a teacher and principal in Lumberton, took center stage after the public forum. The school system, he contended, was caught in a perfect storm. The geography lesson became a poster child for what many thought was wrong with CSCOPE, an online curriculum the school system did use, but something Peters did not use for her lesson on Islam. He talked about the harsh criticism, abusive language, and verbal and physical threats that faculty and staff had endured but he also catered to some people's concerns that Christianity was taking a backseat as their children learned about other religions. "People who know me, and I've been here for more than ten years, they know my values, they know my Christian beliefs. They know my love for this school. They know my love for this community," he said.

He reiterated what he had said in the media. "Lumberton is not promoting Islam. It is a major culture of over two billion people. She was teaching the geographical landscape, food, greetings, including clothing," he said. He refuted allegations that Peters had directly referred to the 9/11 terrorists as freedom fighters. His voice rising, he continued: "I do not think the teacher intentionally, subversively tried to promote Islam or convert students in any way, form, or fashion or did anything wrong." In closing, he read an e-mail from a Lumberton High School 1998 graduate who had taken the class. He did not reveal the name, but Peters, who had the same letter, connected me to the student, Carol Cucio, now in her early thirties and head of visitor services at the Texas state history museum in Austin. Cucio wrote about how Peters's class affected her and how even fifteen years ago Peters had done the same activities. For the first time, a teacher exposed her to other cultures, something Cucio craved as a teen because she had lived in southeast Texas since birth and her family did not travel during her childhood.

Cucio, who took the class in 1995 as a freshman, tried on a black abaya with a veil that left only an opening for the eyes. She also tried on sombreros when they studied Mexico. "Your class opened my eyes to a whole new world and is part of the reason I went on to join the Peace Corps back in 2006," she wrote in the letter. By the spring of 2013, she had traveled to more than thirteen countries and she planned to see more. In the letter, she thanked Peters for giving her and other students the chance to realize that the world held more than Lumberton, the state of Texas, and America. "Teaching cultural understanding helps to facilitate a desire to achieve peace between not only nations, but between neighbors," Valastro read as he quoted Cucio's letter. He let those words sink in, then gave a final plea: "All I ask is give us a chance to teach our kids. Thank you."

On my visit to Lumberton I met with the mother who had spoken at the board meeting about her concerns after seeing her daughter wearing the burka in the Facebook photo. The mother and her daughter sat across from me in a booth at Southern Maid Donuts, another restaurant on Lumberton's main street. The fifteen-year-old had dropped out of Lumberton High in March 2013, about a month after the photo went viral. She was now being home-schooled, using a curriculum developed by former presidential candidate Ron Paul, who incorporated study of the Bible in some of the courses. The teen, who wore her long, platinum-blonde hair in a braid, outwardly seemed like someone who had been a member of the in crowd at Lumberton. She rattled off her activities with confidence. She was a member of the Raiderettes drill team that performed at football games, the Spanish club, and student council. But when she talked about Peters's class, the teen seemed less sure of herself. She wavered on whether she thought her teacher had done anything wrong and took care to say she had gone into the classroom and given Peters a hug after the news hit. During the class, Peters had laid out the various clothing items and then handed the burka to the teen and said, "Here, put it on." At just five feet, the girl was shorter than her peers, the right size for the child-sized item. Her teacher did not force her to try on the burka but putting it on was a little weird. She didn't think much of it until she got home and saw the picture of herself and others on Facebook.[30]

Her reservations about the clothing exercise and the lesson grew after she got home. Her parents, upset about seeing their daughter in the photo, sat her down and showed her a video about a Muslim woman who was whipped for wearing pants. The teen began to feel duped into putting on the burka without really knowing its history and reputation as a sign of oppression. Her mother felt the school should have informed parents about the exercise before their children tried on the outfits. She had grown up in Lumberton and married when she was eighteen and her husband was twenty-three, and had not known that her daughter and other students were even learning about other religions in public school. The thirty-six-year-old was surprised that a school would teach such a touchy subject, and hearing about the lesson's content disturbed her. Seeing a photo of her daughter in a burka upset her even more. She and her husband wanted their kids to grow up with a strong sense of independence, to go to college and have careers, and they hated seeing their daughter wearing what they saw as a symbol of oppression.

Her daughter didn't like that her teacher had just given them a half page of material about Christianity, much less than for other religions. The teen was apprehensive about the idea of learning about other religions, particularly Islam. Because of 9/11, she was uncomfortable hearing about Islam, so much so that she did not think it should be introduced and accepted in the schools as part of the curriculum. Yet, despite her discomfort, she said she understood that Peters was trying to teach them why Muslim women wore the burka. Her mother, however, did not and compared the lessons to a kind of brainwashing: "I feel their goal is to try to make future generations more comfortable with Islam than older generations are. I don't think they are exactly truthful about what Islamic beliefs are. I don't want any of my kids to become Islamic."

The mother's comments seemed to make the teen reverse course in her opinions once more. Since Muslims wouldn't learn about Christianity in their countries, why should Americans have to learn about Islam here? she mused. "I think it's making us very vulnerable. I feel uncomfortable with Muslims in the White House."

"Muslims in the White House?" I asked. "Who do you mean?"

"The president could be," she said.

Rumors had run rampant for years that President Barack Obama was a Muslim. I noted that it had been well established that Obama was Christian. Well, the teen said, the lesson that day simply gave her an uneasy feeling. After the photo went viral, other students teased her because she was the one in the blue burka. Some students called her an "attention whore." To avoid the teasing, she began spending most of the school day in the office. Her mother's reason for pulling her child out of the high school went deeper than her daughter's discomfort. She and her husband did not agree with what the public schools were teaching their child. They worried that their daughter was getting too limited a depiction of Islam in that geography class. The day before I met the mother and daughter in the doughnut shop, Muslim terrorists struck an upscale shopping mall in Nairobi, Kenya, killing more than sixty and injuring 150 others. According to news reports, they targeted non-Muslims. "I do have worries," the mother told me, referring to the Kenya attacks. "What if this is the thing that the Bible warned us about, when religious zealots will kill Christians and say it is the will of God?" She cited John 16: 2–4, which in part reads, "They shall put you out of the synagogues: yea, the time cometh, that whosoever killeth you will think that he doeth God service."[31] She could not understand why people could be okay with instruction about Islam and not with instruction about Christianity. Maybe, rather than taking a class in school, children could learn about Islam and other religions on the Internet, the mother suggested.

Her daughter said she would always be cautious in regard to Islam and Muslims. She didn't want to be hateful but that religion, in her view, was just different.

"Would you ever want to see the inside of a mosque?" I asked.

She shook her head. "I don't care to. I don't believe even remotely in what they believe."

Her comments made me sad that she had dropped out of school to study at home. Her school was at least trying to fill in students' knowledge gap about the world's religions. In general, most Americans don't know much about the major world religions, including their own. In a 2010 survey of adults age eighteen and older, the typical respondent answered only half of the thirty-two questions correctly. Just 45 percent correctly identified Friday as the start of the Jewish Sabbath. A little more than half knew that the Koran was the holy book of Islam and that Ramadan was the Islamic holy month. Barely half knew that the Dalai Lama was a Buddhist. Americans were just as ignorant when asked to identify the faith that has the deities Vishnu and Shiva. The answer? Hinduism. One of the toughest questions: What is the religion of most people in Indonesia, Islam, Hinduism, Buddhism, or Christianity? Just 27 percent got that one right.[32] The answer: Islam.

Zachary Kellas, who took Peters's class a year before the burka incident, understood the importance of his teacher's lessons. He had the opposite reaction of the girl who thought it best not to learn about Islam. Seeing Peters's class unfairly depicted on TV led him to speak at the board meeting. Zachary, who is Catholic, told me that he had learned that Islam had similarities with Christianity and stemmed from Judaism and Christianity. Yet, as Zachary spoke in his living room, his father, Steve Kellas, shook his head. The fifty-four-year-old had traveled to Kuwait and Pakistan and lived there for four weeks at a time as a rig manager for the H&P drilling company. He saw women wearing clothing so restrictive that it hindered their vision. He did not think the geography teacher sugarcoated her discussion on Islam, but he disagreed with some of the opinions his son had developed. His son could have his opinion, and the father said he would hang onto his because he had seen things overseas that his son had not. "I've had actual boots on the ground," Steve Kellas told me. And yet the father was proud that his son thought outside of the box for Lumberton.

On the living room wall, Zachary's parents displayed many of his honors, including a National Honor Society plaque and a letter from President Obama for a youth service award. In between school activities he works with his father on the family's bee farm to raise money for college. In the driveway sat the 2012 Chevy Silverado truck his parents had given him for his recent sixteenth birthday. His BB gun, which he uses to shoot squirrels that mess with the trash, rested in the corner by the front door. His father, intent on introducing me to Texas culture, showed the screen saver on his laptop—a photo of Zachary with his rifle. Then he played a video of Zachary hitting an exploding target.

Islam's bad reputation, Zachary contended, came from the 9/11 attacks as well as from Muslim terrorists around the world. But he refused to look at all Muslims the same way. He credited Peters's class with preparing him for traveling and hoped it would make him a tourist who would never disrespect someone out of ignorance. For that matter, learning about Islam could come in handy even in southeast Texas, given that neighboring Beaumont had a few mosques. But he had no idea if any Muslims attended his high school. If he were Muslim, he probably wouldn't admit it to anyone at Lumberton High, he said.

Lumberton, his mother, Kathy Kellas, added, "was just not very . . ." She paused, and Zachary suggested "tolerant." No, his mother said. "Not very multicultured."

"Redneck," Steve Kellas said and laughed. During my stay in Lumberton, the Kellas family wouldn't take no for an answer when they offered me one of their extra tickets to attend the homecoming football game. At the community pep rally and carnival that week, they nudged me to try gumbo, a mix of rice, chicken, and sausage billed as a slightly spicy dish that paid homage to the area's Cajun influence. "Slightly spicy" may depend on the sensitivity of one's palate; I might have labeled it three-alarm. Yards away, kids threw baseballs at a target, hoping to dunk a football player, and fishing club members gave out prizes to kids who could cast and touch a target on a mat. Superintendent Valastro, in a button-down shirt and football tie, mingled with the crowd. Kathy Kellas tried to connect me with another family who had supported Peters. They refused to meet me. At one point Kathy whispered to me that a few people had urged her not to talk to me. She laughed at the idea of being afraid to talk. She wanted others to know that her family supported the teacher's intent to give her students a look at the rest of the world.

Lumberton teachers' jobs got harder in the aftermath of burkagate. The school system's support of Peters gave the teachers confidence that they could still teach about religion but the hostility from the public also spooked the educators, making them realize how delicate a dance they had to perform around the topic. Skinner, who spoke out in support of her colleague at the board meeting, met with me over dinner at Novrozsky's, a hamburger joint with quirky décor, including a picture of Elvis on one wall and a "Slow Children at Play" sign on another. Skinner was more careful now to articulate her goals when a lesson referenced a religion. She recounted what had happened during a recent class. "You guys know I'm not teaching you Sunday school. I'm teaching you this so you can understand what Puritans believed culturally and religiously," she told her literature class as they studied *The Scarlet Letter.* A student spoke up: "Mrs. Skinner, are you saying that because of the burka thing that happened last year?" She was.

Skinner's views of teaching about Islam are complicated. She was born in Beaumont, raised a Baptist, and has lived in Texas for all of her forty-three years. She could empathize with some parents who worried about teachers stacking the deck in favor of Islam because they were afraid of hurting the feelings of or causing a backlash against Muslims. Or they were worried about being politically incorrect. There could, Skinner said, be some truth to that. Educators should not sugarcoat the facts about a religion but neither should they promote one over another. Skinner did not worry only about the reactions of devout Christians. She also had a Muslim girl in her English class and didn't want to offend her either. The girl was the first Muslim student I had heard of being in Lumberton schools. I asked Skinner if she would ask the teen to meet with me. The teacher said she would try. Skinner, who often followed up our conversations with texts or e-mails with more explanation, was intent on showing that Lumberton did not speak with one voice. Some people had open minds in the town. The Muslim voice, though, was absent during the furor over the burka. No Muslims spoke out at the board meeting or sent e-mails. I wanted to know whether the girl was offended by her peers trying on a burka and the other outfits. Skinner was as eager as I to know the answer. She hadn't thought about that possibility. The teacher had seen trying on a burka as a creative way to open dialogue among students.

Lumberton school officials tapped Brad McBride, the high school's world history teacher, to teach advanced world geography after Peters retired. Peters, whose classroom was next door to McBride's, saw it as a political pick because McBride was known as a devout Baptist. She said, though, that she knew McBride, who had supported her throughout the ordeal, would be unbiased. McBride, who coaches three sports, had not sought the job nor had he asked for another new assignment: teaching two sections of Bible history. Peters thought the school district appeased the community by bringing back a class about the Bible. To her, offering Bible history in 2013–14 was like saying, "Oh, by the way, now we're teaching the Bible class. We are religious. Please," she said, stretching the word into *puh-lease*, "give me a break."

The superintendent talked around the issue of whether returning the Bible courses to Lumberton was a response to the concerns people had raised about Peters's class. Yes, he said, he had told the community during the controversy that if enough students showed interest, the high school would restore a Bible course. And they did. McBride drew twenty-six students to one section and thirteen to another. But it wasn't as if the course was new to Lumberton. A few years before, a literature teacher had taught a course on the Bible in literature, but after she retired, the school district eliminated the course as part of budget cuts. When he was the high school's principal, Valastro pushed for the Bible history class because he knew that so many historical and literary references could be linked to the Bible. Lumberton may be majority Christian, but not all students came to school with a strong knowledge of the Bible or of their religion. I asked Valastro directly whether Peters was right, or whether Valastro was just trying to appease an upset community with these classes. "I definitely wasn't trying to appease anyone," he said, but added that he was taking a lot of heat. The community's culture was conservative Christian and many people were questioning whether he was Christian.[33]

Neither Valastro nor McBride saw the Bible courses as a way to bring back Christianity into the schools. What happened to Peters shook McBride as much as it did other colleagues. He had taught a little about other religions in his world history classes and the burka incident made him more careful. Now, he prefaced what he said about other religions with caveats like "This is what they say" or "This is what they believe." He became more aware that students or parents could misinterpret what he said, he told me between classes at the high school. He told students he was not offering an opinion when he said that Muslims believe Jesus was a respected scholar, even a prophet, but did not see him as the son of God. He was simply describing Muslim beliefs. The teacher, who was once a sports reporter, believed he had to emphasize exactly what he was doing, more than he thought was reasonable. Burkagate had changed everything.

Frustration seeped into his voice. He not only respected Peters, he knew from a good source that the teacher gave all major religions fair treatment. His son took Peters's advanced geography classes and came home two weeks before the burka incident asking questions about Christian doctrine that Peters had discussed. Others had accused her of not doing much on Christianity, a bogus accusation in McBride's view. "Did you happen to see that photo that caused the outcry?" he asked me. "Did you see what was in the background on the board? Judaism, Christianity, and Islam. All three are covered." In the fall of 2013 he was covering the same ground Peters had the previous school year, but he used PowerPoint presentations rather than hands-on activities as teaching tools. He didn't own a collection of Middle Eastern clothing. What if he did, I asked? Would he let students try on a burka? "At this point, I sure wouldn't," he said, laughing a little.

In his geography and world history classes, McBride set ground rules, prohibiting name-calling or degradation of other faiths. When he taught about Islam he heard a common question from students: "Why do they all hate us over there?" McBride told his students they were trying to paint all Muslims with the same brush because of what they heard on the news about terrorists. But not all Muslims, he said, acted that way. In fact, he told his students that there were some Muslims they would be fine being friends with at Lumberton High. That did not mean the students had to agree with Muslims' beliefs. McBride's caution in teaching about religion also spread to his Bible as history class. I had asked to see the class in action, but school district officials said no. They drew the line at letting me talk to students in the school or see the classes.

On its own, teaching the Bible history class was a daunting assignment for McBride because no one gave him a curriculum. McBride spent the summer crafting his own curriculum with the help of a Bible, world history texts, and a Christian website that drew from many versions of the Bible. He looked for ways to connect the history of Israel and the Roman Empire to passages in the Bible and planned to focus on the Old Testament during the first semester and the New Testament during the second. The class focuses on history but McBride saw it as providing literacy on the Bible as well. He would take his students through a list of biblical allusions provided in a study guide for the Advanced Placement English exam. The students would learn, for example, the origin of such expressions as "An eye for an eye, a tooth for a tooth."

In the hopes of preventing any problems with the Bible courses, he sent a letter home to students and their parents. In the letter, he talked about the separation of church and state and how tricky it can be to balance freedom *of* religion with freedom *from* religion.

He cited state standards on the Bible courses, which required that he follow federal and state guidelines on maintaining religious neutrality and accommodating the diverse religious views and traditions of students. "Teachers of this course are repeatedly directed not to proselytize," he wrote. In another paragraph, he wrote that he thought it was best to avoid speculation about his own religion. "I am a Christian, and my family is a mixture of Protestant and Catholic. I have attended church my entire life," the forty-two-year-old teacher wrote. "I do not expect denominational issues to be a cause for your concern." He called for an atmosphere of respect, noting that the class would likely lead students to identify their particular religious beliefs but that he would not require them to reveal their religion, denomination, or religious viewpoints. McBride's goal was simple: prevent another blow-up over religion in Lumberton. When he teaches the Bible class, he couches what he says to present himself as unbiased in much the same way he does in geography. He uses phrases like "the Bible says" rather than the words "This is what I believe." He acknowledged it could be awkward for him. "When you're teaching Bible history, you're going to cover the stories, and some people don't believe them. I do," he said.

Behind McBride on the classroom whiteboard was a handwritten announcement: "See You at the Pole @ 7:15 a.m." On the fourth Wednesday of every September, Christian students gather around the flagpoles at their schools for a before-school prayer meeting, a nationwide event created in 1990 by Christian teens at a Texas high school.[34] One of McBride's Bible history students wrote the notice but the teacher had reservations about advertising the event. He wondered whether it would appear that students were being pressured to attend. He decided to let the invitation stay. The prayer rally was set for the next morning. No one was at the main flagpole in front of the school, though, when I got there the next day. I texted Skinner, whose twins were planning to sing at the event, and she said the event was behind the school by the football field's flagpole. She was heading there to hear her daughters. Skinner had grown up in the Christian culture in southeast Texas and saw Christianity's presence at the school as normal and legal—as long as students were the ones pushing the practices.

At the flagpole near the football field, Skinner stood toward the back among a group of roughly forty. It was already a sticky 90 degrees. Several youths wore Raiders 4 Christ T-shirts. "Jesus is alive, and oh, happy day, happy day, you wash my sins away," two boys sang as they played guitar. In the back of the group, one of two pastors there from the Calvary Baptist Church stretched his arm out as if he were extending it to the heavens. "Yes, Lord, yes, Lord," prayed the pastor, whose black T-shirt further showed his religious fervor with the words "The gates of Hell will not prevail." Skinner's twins soon stood next to the guitarists and sang Christian folk and pop songs. "Blessed be the name of the lord, Blessed be the name of the lord, . . . Blessed be the name Jesus," the pair sang. Other students from the school drove into the nearby lot in pickups and SUVs or stepped off school buses as the prayer rally continued. During his sermon, a student pastor from Calvary Baptist praised the students for their bravery that morning. "The world we live in is broken. It's infected with sin," he said, reading a sermon from his iPad. "It takes a lot of boldness to stand here as your peers are driving by. . . . The world we live in is broken, but the remedy is Jesus Christ. As his people, as people who bear his name, as you talk to your friends, what kind of stories are you telling in Jesus's name?"

When the forty-five-minute event ended, the students posed for photos that later appeared on the Calvary Student Ministries Facebook page. I spoke with Steven Hays, a pastor who stood at the back. Hays, as we began talking about the burka dress-up incident, noted he had written a paper about Islam versus Christianity as part of his pastoral studies. He said he was worried about what had happened in the high school's geography classroom. After studying material about Islam and traveling the world, he had come to believe that Christianity truly was the best option. He had seen far too many people deceived by false ideology. "For example, with Islam, it's completely a satanic deception," he said, adding that the final word in the Bible was settled long before Mohammed was a player. Islam, he noted, denied that Jesus was the son of God. I refrained from inserting that Jews, too, did not believe Jesus was the son of God, or that Jesus had little or no significance within many of the world's religions. "The truth of Christianity is undeniable," Hays said as we moved from the football field to the edge of the parking lot by our cars. His four-year-old son ran around nearby. Hays thought Peters went too far letting students try on a burka, especially if she did not do the same exercise for each religion. He also worried about the effect on students who felt they had to don the clothing. "Educate but don't embarrass," he said.

What, I wondered, would he have students try on to represent Christianity? "Wear normal clothes because it's the normal thing," he said.

Very shortly, he said, he will travel on a mission to Muslim countries to attempt to convert others to Christianity. As we were about to say goodbye, he asked me, "Do you know Jesus as your savior?" I had not, at any time in our conversation, revealed that I was not Christian. I smiled and dodged the query. "Uh, let's not go there. I'd like to just be a journalist here."

He nodded. "Okay, see you. I wish you the best of luck." I knew he did not represent all of the Christian clergy in Lumberton. I had spent a few hours with a different pastor at a nearby Baptist church, the one that McBride attended. That pastor never spouted anti-Islam rhetoric. Nor did he try to convert me. He, in fact, saw the beauty in what Peters had tried to do.

Two days later, Skinner texted me: the Muslim family had agreed to talk. I called the student's mother. I could interview her daughter that afternoon with a caveat. Her daughter did not want me to reveal the family members' names out of fear that people would target them. She would graduate from Lumberton High in 2014 but her parents still planned to live there. They had lived in Lumberton for more than twenty years, but not everyone knew they were Muslim. The girl's mother, a native of Kingsville, Texas, was white and had been raised Catholic; she converted to Islam six or seven years after she married a Muslim man from Jordan. The girl, with long, curly black hair and pale skin, and her mother could walk through Lumberton and no one would single them out. The teen wore a hijab only when she entered a mosque. She did not put it on for school out of fear of ridicule.[35]

The girl, a seventeen-year-old senior, spoke with me at a table in the family's kitchen. Her mother brought us tall glasses of water, then joined us. So did the girl's twenty-year-old brother, a commuter student at nearby Lamar University with still-recent memories of attending Lumberton High. There was nothing in their sparsely decorated home that indicated they were Muslim other than a few Korans on the dining room table. The girl said she used to be scared that people would see the holy books when they came to the house and deduce that the family was Muslim. I did not get to meet the girl's father, who was working at the gas station he co-owns with another Jordanian. The family moved to Lumberton because it was closer to the gas station and because the schools had a good reputation. The girl's parents did not know of Lumberton's reputation as a white-flight town. The girl began feeling isolated and different as early as third grade, when she heard other children make derogatory references to Muslims. Rather than say anything, she chose not to reveal her religion.

When she reached high school, it became harder to stay silent, especially after her ninth-grade geography teacher made prejudicial comments about Muslims and implied that they were all terrorists. That teacher later went to work for another school system. One day in class the students watched a video about a girl named Esma, and the teacher said with a grin to the students, "What is that, 'Asthma'?" He made fun of the name, which was the name of one of the girl's cousins. She tried to get the teacher to show more respect. She told him her family was Muslim but that did not help. He then asked her what her family was, "Are they Sunni or are they shitty?" The girl felt the teacher was purposely mispronouncing "Shi'a" or "Shiite." She and her family members are Sunnis. Her freshman year, she often came home from school in tears or angry. It wasn't just her teacher who made the slights. Her peers did too when they found out she was Muslim. "Do you have a bomb in your backpack?" a schoolmate asked her one day.

She did not know Peters and had not known about the burka exercise until she saw it on the television news. Her first reaction was that she could not understand what was wrong with trying on the garments. But she was not sure how she would have felt if she were in the class and saw a non-Muslim girl try on the burka or a hijab. In the Facebook photo, several students were grinning. She might have been offended if students were making fun. She had seen peers don a scarf and then say, "Don't kill me." The day before we met, a friend of hers wrapped a scarf around her head so only her eyes were show-ing. Another friend took a photo, posted it on Twitter, and made a headline that read "Twin or terrorist," because it was twin day at the high school, a spirit event the school ran before a football game. The girl told these stories in a soft tone. She kept thanking me for being there. She had never had the chance to really talk about what it was like to be one of just a few Muslims in her school.

Friends have asked the girl if she really wants to be Muslim. A female student once tried to convert her brother, telling him Chris-tianity was the only way to go. He let the girl talk. His father had advised him that learning about other religions was a good thing. It was as if I were hearing myself from more than thirty years ago when the Muslim girl talked about going to her brother's gradua-tion and chafing as prayers were said in "Jesus's name." Then she had to sit through another prayer in Jesus's name when she was inducted into the school's National Honor Society chapter. She looked around rather than bow her head to join a prayer that was not from her religion. Her refusal to participate, of course, made her stick out more. Christian prayers were delivered at both of my older brothers' high school graduations.

For Skinner's class that fall, the girl wrote an essay titled "Where Do I Fit In?" She described herself as half American and half Arab. "I love my heritage, but sometimes I feel like I do not fit in anywhere," she wrote. "I have dealt with prejudice from people everywhere my whole life." American friends started to treat her differently when they found out she was Muslim and half Arab. When she attended social gatherings for Arabs, she sensed that others were judging her because she did not blend in with her extremely light skin. When she visited her father's family in Jordan, she also drew stares. "No matter where I fit, I am proud of who I am," she wrote in the concluding sentences. "I judge people individually because 'bad' people come from all races and religions. Luckily, good people do, too." It was hurtful, she said, to read comments on articles denigrating Muslims in the aftermath of the burka incident. But there was something positive for her in the burka controversy: finding out that Peters was Jewish. That made her happy because it confronted another stereotype, that all Jews and Muslims hate each other because of differences over Israel.

In one news report the superintendent had said that Peters was Jewish, hoping to dispel the notion that the teacher was trying to convert students to Islam. Peters wished the superintendent had never mentioned her religion because she thought it was irrelevant. A good teacher, regardless of his or her faith, should be able to teach about religion without proselytizing. As a teacher, she had tried to fight the attitudes of students, parents, and a community. "I may go to my grave still distraught about it," she said of the uproar over her class. A year after I met Peters at her home in Lumberton, she started cleaning out some of her old teaching materials. She saw the reusable bags with the Middle Eastern clothing, grabbed them, and threw them into a pile on top of leaves in her backyard. She ignited the pile with a cigarette lighter and watched as flames destroyed the abaya, burka, hijab, and even the white Saudi Arabian clothing for males she had sewed herself. It took an hour for the clothing to turn into ash. She stared at the remains and saw them as symbolic of so much, including her anger about recent beheadings by Islamic militant groups and about the way people responded to a lesson meant to open minds, not close them. That pile of ash was black, this bottomless abyss of black, she told me in a firm voice still tinged with bitterness. She had tried not to look back too much since she retired from Lumberton High, but it was hard. Her last year was a dark time that convinced her that her town did not want to allow teachers to open their children's minds to the world.[36]

Valastro, the schools superintendent, refused to be so pessimistic when he met with me during one of my last days in Lumberton. He knew the 9/11 attacks and other terroristic acts instilled fear in people, but he also recognized the need to teach students to not view all Muslims as terrorists. If their parents believed that, then they were perpetuating Islamophobia and creating yet a whole new level of racism, he said. "You need to understand that as a whole in every sector of society, in every religion, you're going to have a variety of forms. Look at the Ku Klux Klan. Are they not Christian? Look at the white supremacists. Are they not Christians and think if you're not blond-haired, blue-eyed, you should be wiped off the face of the earth? It's just constant," said the trim, gray-haired schools chief, who revealed little emotion as he spoke.

He thought Lumberton could continue to teach about the world's religions but would also have to continue to deal with the phobia some people had of Muslims. Over the next few decades, Valastro predicted, Lumberton schools would teach even more about different religions as part of geography and history because the United States was becoming more religiously diverse. He saw such a need for it, especially when he read news stories about the 2013 Miss America, Nina Davuluri. People targeted her as a Muslim when she was in fact Hindu. He was not surprised to hear that a Lumberton student thought President Obama was Muslim because a large percentage of Americans thought that too. He figured they were mixing up Osama Bin Laden with Obama.

But he also saw no change in the school system's embrace of its majority Christian community. The superintendent, who's Catholic, prided himself on being an educator for twenty-eight years and maintaining himself visibly as a Christian. He contended he could hold both roles and advocate for a well-rounded education. I asked about the two Christian crosses set on a table to the side of his desk. He smiled and pointed out a few more behind me. His secretaries gave him the crosses, including two that doubled as bookends, for Christmas, Boss's Day, and on other occasions. He saw nothing wrong with having Christian symbols in a public school superintendent's office. "That's what I am. I think you need to be who you are. Just because I'm Catholic, I'm Christian, I don't think that impedes me from doing my job."

But how would seeing those crosses resonate with a parent or student who wanted to protest an overtly Christian practice in Lumberton schools? Say, for example, they wanted to stop prayer at graduations or football games. Valastro saw it as a nonissue. No one had challenged those traditions unless he counted the Wisconsin group's complaint about the kindergarten graduation. The superintendent talked to the principal and reminded him that such prayers must be student-led to stay within the law.

"How does a five-year-old make a decision on whether to lead?" I asked.

He smiled. "Their prayer might be more meaningful than ours. They say it from the heart."

As the mother of a kindergartner at that time, I wondered how such young children could come up with the idea for graduation prayer themselves. An adult would have to plant the idea. Valastro had no problem with what the principal did. "You've talked to people. You've been here," he said. "It's a little bit different here in the South."

Staring at those crosses, I silently agreed.

CHAPTER TWO

Did a Field Trip Put Students in the Lion's Den?

STRANGERS WERE SPEWING venom at Wellesley Middle School. It was the fall of 2010, and the school was in the news for taking its sixth graders on a field trip to a mosque. It wasn't the Lumberton story that first led me to explore how schools were handling religion in the twenty-first century. It was my childhood experiences and this mosque field trip by a school in Wellesley, a well-heeled Boston suburb not far from my town.

As the afternoon prayer began, a handful of boys apparently had knelt, prostrated, and prayed with a line of male worshippers.[1] That the mosque in question had been accused of having financial backers and a founder with terrorist ties fueled the vitriol. "How idiotic to take our precious little ones into the lion's den!" a reader wrote in a comment on a local article.[2] The news coverage caught my attention but not because I was worried about middle school students entering a mosque. I was intrigued and envious. I did not learn about other religions in my own childhood. I also had never set foot inside a mosque.

39

Roughly two hundred sixth graders from Wellesley's sole public middle school went on the field trip to a mosque in Roxbury, near downtown Boston, as part of a required social studies class called Enduring Beliefs and the World Today. For Wellesley, it was the school's first trip to this particular mosque in the heart of Boston, but for several years sixth graders had visited another mosque and a Jewish temple as a part of the world religions class. They also learned about Christianity and Hinduism, often with the help of guest speakers. No one had complained about the class until the spring 2010 field trip. Unbeknownst to the school, a mother who was chaperoning videoed the boys who had taken part in the prayer and later gave her film to an outside group, which created a video castigating the school and the mosque titled "Wellesley, Massachusetts Public School Students Learn to Pray to Allah."

The roughly ten-minute film, with narration by an unidentified male and a woman who was reenacting the voice of one of the mother chaperones, was released three months after the field trip. The video began with footage of the call to prayer at the mosque and listeners could hear a woman off-screen, apparently the videographer, whispering, "Oh, my God" as the camera showed a handful of Wellesley sixth-grade boys in the line of worshippers. The male narrator, in a deep, polished voice, said (as ominous-sounding piano music swelled), "On May 25, 2010, students from the Wellesley, Massachusetts, public middle school were taken on a field trip to the Muslim American Society's mosque. During their visit, students were asked to participate in the Muslim midday prayer. Several Wellesley public school boys took part. How did Wellesley school teachers allow this to happen?" At first, the video focused on the field trip and the mother's reaction to seeing the boys pray. Then it segued into a commentary on the mosque and allegations that it had ties to prominent terrorist groups. The female narrator talked about how the mosque had promoted wife beating in some of its literature. The video ended with the male narrator saying that our institutions were failing us and public schools must not allow the Muslim American Society to proselytize to our students. School and mosque officials called the video a slick piece of propaganda created by the Boston-based Americans for Peace and Tolerance. The group's leader, Charles Jacobs, also a columnist for the Boston-based *Jewish Advocate*, had long alleged that the mosque's financial backers had ties to radical Islam, a claim that mosque officials continue to refute. School district officials said they didn't know about the boys praying until they saw the video, but did not believe the mosque, as an entity, had encouraged the students to join the worshippers. They also were not concerned about past allegations about the mosque, noting that it was common for such accusations about terrorism to be tossed around when Islam was involved.

The incident nonetheless raised questions about Wellesley's course and about whether the school should continue the field trips. Wellesley Middle School's social studies chair had worked hard to set up a trip to the Roxbury mosque. He did not see previous allegations about the mosque as a reason not to visit the most majestic example of a Muslim house of worship in the Boston area. The mosque, in the heart of an urban neighborhood, was known for drawing Muslims of different races and backgrounds and could teach students that a starkly different, diverse world existed not far from Wellesley's borders.[3] Called the Islamic Society of Boston Cultural Center, the 68,000-square-foot mosque complex is roughly 10,000 square feet larger than a football field and includes a café, shop, and Islamic elementary school. From the outside, with its black dome and red-brick tower called a minaret, the mosque has a palatial look. Yet, with brick and limestone similar to those at nearby Roxbury Community College, the Islamic center also blends into the neighborhood, an intentional part of the design. The mosque sits on Malcolm X Boulevard, and beneath the street sign is Malcolm X's Muslim name, el-Hajj Malik el-Shabazz. El-Hajj honors Malcolm X's pilgrimage to Mecca, one of the five pillars, or obligations, that a Muslim must fulfill.[4]

The woman who led the Wellesley group through the mosque in May 2010 was a veteran tour guide who converted to Islam from Christianity in her twenties. She agreed to recount what happened on the tour for me provided I did not use her name. She feared retaliation by anti-Muslim groups. Wearing a hijab and a long dress, the guide greeted the roughly two hundred students, teachers, and parent chaperones and ushered them into the mosque's enclosed courtyard. The group was at least five times the size of a typical tour group at the mosque, and the guide and school officials had planned a program to accommodate the many students. The visitors mostly dressed in long pants and long-sleeve shirts, heeding school instructions to keep their skin covered. They did not have to cover their heads, though female visitors usually wrap a scarf around their hair out of respect. Typical of any mosque, there were no pictures of Mohammed, the central figure of Islam, inside. The building, with its high ceilings and cavernous space, had few adornments, save for signs in Arabic and English. But students immediately could sense they were in a holy place. One sign on a wall, labeled "Morality," quoted a passage from the Koran: "God commands justice and excellence and giving to relatives, and he forbids indecency, and wickedness, and oppression. . . . He admonishes you that you may take heed."

From the courtyard the guide led the Wellesley students into the social hall, just behind the worship hall. Sitting in chairs, the students listened as the guide gave a half-hour presentation on Islam, talking about the religion's core beliefs and practices. In the video shot by the parent chaperone, listeners hear the guide, who's using the microphone and speaking in a matter-of-fact tone, tell the group, "You have to believe in Allah, and Allah is the one God, the only one worthy of worship, all-forgiving, all-merciful, wise, knowing. Everything we do is to please God because God has guided us to do things." But a key phrase was cut, a news release from mosque officials later said. At the start, the guide said, "To be a Muslim, you have to believe." The cut-and-paste job on the video manipulated the guide's words and made it appear as if she were "telling students that *they* have to believe,"[5] the mosque's news release said. The lecture was merely a lesson about what Muslims believe. Wellesley school officials concurred that there was nothing improper in the presentation, but also added that they coached students to listen with a critical ear. The guide gave her perspective. The students' jobs were to learn and to do exactly what they did after the guide finished her talk: they asked her questions as she walked around the social hall, looking for raised hands.

The guide also quizzed the students on their knowledge of Islam and they impressed her with how much they already knew, including the parts of the mosque, such as the mihrab, the concaved niche in a wall that all Muslims face when they pray. The mihrab points in the direction of the sacred house, the Kaaba, in Mecca. The students knew, too, that the minaret, the tower on top of the mosque, was where someone stood to call Muslims to start prayer. In the Roxbury mosque the minaret was symbolic. To announce the start of prayer, a man chanted into a microphone in front of the mihrab, and the sound of him singing a mixture of trills and long notes in Arabic reverberated off the high ceilings.[6]

On the video the female narrator made it seem as if evil were occurring as the call to prayer began. "Miseducating students about Islamic history was one thing, but what the mosque and school did next was totally inappropriate," the narrator said. After the guide's talk, the narrator contended, all women chaperones and the girls were asked to leave the prayer area and the boys were asked to stay. Mosque officials said the video again warped what had happened. Yes, women and men prayed in separate areas, but during the tour, when a group of girls and boys asked to watch the prayer, the guide instructed them to sit off to the side. There was no intentional segregation of the sexes in the middle school tour group, according to the mosque's news release.[7]

The mother with the video camera looked up and saw five middle school boys praying with the line of worshippers. The boys stood shoulder to shoulder with dozens of men, some African, some immigrants from Pakistan, Saudi Arabia, and Indonesia, some white.[8] "I was shaking as I saw one of the Jewish boys pray," the actress playing the mother said on the video. "I looked at one of the teachers to say something, do something. No one said anything. I wanted to get out quickly and go home."[9] The video intimated that the mosque instigated the praying by school students. But the invitation to pray happened casually, according to Jackson Posnik, one of the boys. After the guide's lecture the students split into small groups and visited booths set up in a large hall. Jackson tried out oils on his hands and had his name written in Arabic while other youths looked at books and scarves or read essays by children about what it was like to be Muslim in America. At one point, Jackson and four other boys stood near a male member of the mosque. The man, who had a beard and a do-rag on his head, took the boys over to see the mosque prayer clock and pointed out the listing of daily worship times and the date and year on the Islamic calendar. The worship was about to start, he told Jackson and the other boys. "You guys can participate if you'd like," he said.[10]

Jackson, who is Jewish, and the other boys had already visited the *wudu*, the washing station area, and done the ritual hand- and foot-washing. Like the worshippers around them, they were in bare feet. Jackson had no idea where his teacher, Jonathan Rabinowitz, was. He figured Mr. R, as the teacher was nicknamed, was standing at the back of the hall. Jackson had never seen Muslims pray before and did not want to refuse what might be a once-in-a-lifetime opportunity. He and the boys stood near the man, and Jackson didn't see it as praying since he didn't understand the Arabic swirling around him, words that mostly were praise to God. He mimicked what everyone did, standing, bowing, kneeling, and prostrating on the carpeted floor. No one said anything for months until the video surfaced on September 15, four days after the anniversary of the September 11 World Trade Center attacks, a time when anti-Muslim sentiment often rises in the United States. Americans for Peace and Tolerance issued a news release along with the video and the media responded.

The next evening, after a back-to-school night for parents, fly-ers from the group were stuck on parents' cars, alerting them to the video and the mosque trip. As school began the following morning, media trucks filled the area and reporters interviewed parents drop-ping off their children. Jackson and his mother, Calli Posnik, told me months later that they were particularly livid about the Boston group's attack on the middle school and its program. In Jackson's view, no harm was done just because the boys joined the prayer. He thought that people made a big deal of the incident because of their own ignorance about religion, and he was disturbed that so many people thought he and the other boys were being converted to Is-lam or, worse, that the boys were learning "weird things that would make us do suicide bombs," as he put it to me later.[11] His mother was angry at the parent who videotaped her son without permission but not angry at the school or the teachers. To her the controversy was a "mountain of a molehill made by one wacko" and the course was valuable for all sixth graders because they gained knowledge applicable to everyday life. If she had one criticism, it was that she thought the teachers should have said directly to the students be-forehand, "Watch, but don't participate."[12]

First Amendment experts and groups that support the separation of church and state told reporters that the school crossed a line by not keeping all students off to the side during worship. Conserva-tive bloggers and Fox commentators bashed the school for putting students in that situation in the first place. Wellesley schools su-perintendent Bella Wong issued a mea culpa in a letter to parents, explaining that the trip's "purpose was for students to visit and ob-serve a place of worship. It was not the intent for students to be able to participate in any of the religion's practices." That, Wong said, was an error, and she gave her apologies. Many parents, some who deeply valued the program, thought the superintendent did not need to apologize.[13]

About a week after the controversy made the news, Joel Sisen-wine, the senior rabbi at Temple Beth Elohim, the lone Jewish temple in Wellesley, devoted his Friday night sermon to the controversy. He beseeched congregants to stop blaming the group that started the controversy and to recognize that the mosque, the school, the group that made the video, and the videographer had all made mistakes. The rabbi, who had led tours at his temple for Wellesley sixth graders for a decade, said the community should praise the superintendent for her apology, given that it was wrong for students to join the Muslim worshippers in prayer. Blame Jacobs and his group and the mother who took the video, the rabbi said, for using the five boys to make propaganda. But the school system, he added, should have been aware of the past controversies concerning the Roxbury mosque and chosen instead to visit the smaller, lesser-known mosque in the nearby town of Wayland. Still, he lobbied for field trips to continue to houses of worship and told his congregation how he ended each tour. He tells Wellesley students how lucky they are to be able to take such field trips because he never had such an opportunity. He did not enter a church until he was twenty-one.[14]

A few weeks after the mosque field trip made headlines, I called Wellesley Middle School hoping to speak to educators but was told that only the superintendent was taking media calls.

The soft-spoken superintendent told me to call her Bella, as we sat in her office at the back of the middle school complex. An attorney by training, she said there was never any doubt that a mistake was made on the field trip and that students should not have participated in worship. The school got it right in the permission slip by saying students would visit the mosque to see its architecture and observe the call to prayer. "Observe" was the key word. But even as she admitted that the school system erred, Wong felt it had been set up and that a valuable course of study could be hurt in the process.[15] The parent who had taken the video had contacted Americans for Peace and Tolerance before the field trip; that group was a longtime critic of the Roxbury mosque. The group's director,

Charles Jacobs, later acknowledged that the parent was asked to video what had occurred, even as he stood by the criticism of the field trip and the choice of the Roxbury mosque. When he spoke with me, Jacobs reiterated his concerns about what had happened on the field trip. "The five students prayed to Allah," he said. "As Americans, we shouldn't be proselytizing each other's kids. That's just not right for any religion."[16]

Yes, Wong agreed, the children should not have been asked to join the worshippers. And yes, teachers should have better instructed the children before the trip so that they'd know to watch from the sidelines. But going on the field trips was an integral part of the class. Wellesley started designing the course before the 2001–2002 school year, intending to teach about ancient Greece and Rome in the first half of the year and about the world's religions in the second half. The class was in the works months before the 9/11 attacks and before many schools and universities were scurrying to find ways to better teach students about Islam and dispel the growing stereotype among Americans that all Muslims were terrorists or that Islam and its holy book, the Koran, fomented terrorism.

Massachusetts, like most states, calls for teaching about the world's religions in the context of social studies or world geography. In the past, Wellesley had done what most schools systems did: teach about religions sparingly as they came up in the context of world geography. Wellesley took an unusual step for a public school by creating a half-year course on the world's religions for sixth graders and instructing teachers to spend roughly a month each on Judaism, Christianity, and Islam and then three weeks on Hinduism. Students cover seven aspects of each faith, including the stories of the religion's origin, its core beliefs, and its significant leaders. Field trips became a part of the school's way of giving the instruction a contemporary flavor. Wellesley's decision to create the class came from a place of intellectual angst among its educators.[17] Teachers worried that their students did not understand the importance of religion in international politics. At the same time, there was a developmental reason for picking sixth grade for the study of religion. At eleven, twelve, and almost thirteen, students become more judgmental, and this is the age when bullying, teasing, and stereotyping can become rampant. The hope was that by teaching classes about different religions, teachers could prevent ridicule in that area. The age also seemed perfect because many students at that stage celebrate rites of passage in their own religion.

Wellesley was also the right kind of place to experiment with a course about the world's religions. It is home to Wellesley College, a women's institution that has educated two secretaries of State, Hillary Clinton and Madeleine Albright, and it has the groomed, cookie-cutter feel of a town striving for perfection. It was named the country's third-most-educated city in 2013 by NerdWallet, a website that evaluates cities based on census data. Nearly half of the town's residents have a graduate or professional degree, compared with less than a fourth statewide. The mean family income, at $246,146, is more than double the state average, and the town's commercial district reflects its high income.[18] The Kidville store sign touts "Happy Kids, Happy Families," while pricing a sixteen-week art class for two-year-olds at a whopping $445. Other shops include Talbots, known for its preppy clothes, and a store devoted to the elite sport of lacrosse. The town is liberal in leaning, though its embrace of environmental issues has an ironic twist. Every Saturday, residents swarm to the recycling center to drop off recyclables in their gas-guzzling SUVs.[19]

The population of roughly 28,000 is mostly white with a small number of blacks and Hispanics and a slightly larger number of Asians, including immigrants from India.[20] Religiously, data were hard to find, but the houses of worship give a snapshot: most are Protestant churches and a few are Catholic. The Village Church, founded in 1798, dominates the town center with its steeple visible from every corner and a cemetery that stretched across a green. It is a progressive Protestant congregation that prides itself on choosing to have an open and affirming designation, which means the church, a part of the United Church of Christ, is open to all regardless of sexual orientation. The church, loosely referred to as a congregational church, has more than 1,000 members. Temple Beth Elohim, founded in 1949, also is a dominant presence, with 1,100 families. Wayland, a neighboring town, has a mosque. Within the schools, Jewish children talk of being one of a handful per class, at most. Muslims and Hindus said they are usually one of just a few in their entire school.

Wellesley's teachers, as they decided to make religion more central to sixth-grade social studies, also looked through a crystal ball at America's religious makeup. The United States soon could become a minority Protestant country for the first time, and immigration was creating more religious diversity. More Muslims and Hindus in particular were immigrating to America, including to the suburbs of Boston.[21] Wellesley teachers and administrators wanted to give students basic literacy about the world's major religions and whet students' curiosity about other faiths so they would want to learn even more as they grew older. Doing more to teach the students about religion was an imperative, not a luxury. The teachers were also well aware that statistics on how much Americans knew about religion were grim.

After the controversy, Wellesley had to decide whether to return to the mosque in Roxbury, or any mosque. The video came out in September. The next group of sixth graders would not start the class until late January. Religion scholars and First Amendment experts had repeated a common refrain when I talked with them: they said it was unwise to take public school children on field trips to houses of worship. It was too easy for someone to break the line separating church and state if students were in a temple, church, or mosque. One mosque, one Jewish temple, one church could not represent all of the houses of worship of a particular religion. Wouldn't the field trips give students too myopic a view of one religion?

As January 2011 approached and the start of the course neared, I began asking the superintendent to let me into the school to see the program. She said she wasn't comfortable exposing the school to more media coverage but did not give me an outright no. I kept in touch, and she connected me with Adam Blumer, chair of the social studies department. Soon, I at least got permission to visit a class even as the superintendent was unsure about allowing interviews of students. The school was skittish, but I did not find out why until a later conversation with Wong. When the video of the field trip went viral, calls and e-mails from around the country streamed into Wellesley school headquarters and into the middle school. Callers, Wong recalled, made death threats, telling the school secretary that "we should be beheaded, our hands should be cut off, and the building should burn with us inside it."[22] The school reported the death threats to the police and to the FBI, who decided the threats were too general to warrant extra protection. But the superintendent felt that the school was vulnerable and worried that more publicity would escalate the threats and further provoke the group that had released the video.

At the middle school, Blumer became my ally as he got a sense that I wanted to show readers what the class was about and address the concerns that had grown out of the controversy, including some people's belief that sixth grade was far too early for an academic class about religion. Blumer sounded like a missionary when he spoke about the course, so fervent was his belief that sixth grade was the ideal time for it and that learning about religion was a life skill. He was driven by a memory of when he was a teen growing up in Framingham, another Boston suburb. Jewish, he was knowledgeable about his faith but knew next to nothing about other religions. Around age sixteen, he went to a funeral of a friend who was Catholic. When everyone stood to go to the front of the church and accept communion and eat the wafer and drink the wine signifying the body and blood of Christ, Blumer was terrified. Should he stay in his seat or should he join the line? He had no idea. I related to his story. My closest friend, whom I met on the first day of kindergarten, is Catholic. I had accompanied her to mass on occasion. The first time, like Blumer, I felt awkward, unsure whether to kneel when others did and whether to follow my friend and join the line heading to communion. But I was brave enough to ask. She whispered to me that I should stay at my seat. Wellesley's course, Blumer believed, could at least give students enough knowledge to know how to act in different houses of worship.[23]

He was also not naïve. He knew teaching about religion could lead to controversy even in a liberal town in a state considered among the most secular in the country. He created a two-page letter for teachers to send home to parents before the religions unit began. In that letter, he addressed two questions: "Why teach about religion at all? Why teach about it in middle school?" He listed several reasons, including religion's role in culture and its attempt to explain the unexplainable, as well as the school system's goal to teach students respect for human differences. And why middle school? Because that's often when children are wrestling with the kinds of questions religion addresses: "Who am I? How am I unique? How am I part of a larger community? How do good people act? What is bad? Why do seemingly unexplainable things happen?" He gave parents a heads-up about the plan for field trips, describing the excursions as "one of the greatest gifts we can give to students."[24]

From the start, the teachers' challenge had been to make sure the course heeded the line separating church and state but also engaged students. When they taught about Greece in the fall, they let students perform plays and skits. But modern-day religion was a touchier subject. Teachers knew it was unwise to let students reenact religious rituals or create raps about religions. During one of my first meetings with the social studies chair, I also met Jonathan Rabinowitz, who had taught the class since 2002. Rabinowitz was eager to get the full story told about the Wellesley course. He invited me to visit his classes as I waited for the superintendent's permission, which finally came about three weeks after my first visit to the school.

Rabinowitz felt his transition to college had been tougher than it needed to be because of his lack of knowledge about other faiths. Born in South Africa, he moved to the United States at age six and spent most of his youth and early adulthood in a Jewish bubble. He went to a Jewish day school through middle school and mostly socialized with other Jews in Sharon, a suburb on Boston's South Shore. His observant Jewish parents wanted him to stay home on Friday nights, the start of Shabbat, rather than play soccer. When he went to college at McGill University in Montreal, he was uncomfortable discussing religion with others. He did not know how to even ask questions about Jesus Christ. At Wellesley Middle School, he was open with students that he was Jewish and saw his strong Jewish education as a plus because most of his students knew little or nothing about Judaism. For him, it was liberating to watch sixth-grade students have the types of discussions he'd shied away from as a youth.

Rabinowitz also brought bits and pieces to his students from memories of his participation in Beyond Borders, a program that partnered a dozen teachers from Arab countries with a dozen from the United States. First, the group spent two weeks together in Maine in the summer, and the conversations sometimes turned to the Arab teachers' views of Jews in America. Rabinowitz recalled them talking about how they thought or were taught that the 9/11 World Trade Center attacks were organized by Israel or by Jews and that it was not just coincidence that there were no Jews killed in the attacks. (In fact, roughly 10 percent of the victims in the attacks were Jewish.) In his classroom, when the discussion revolved around women's rights in Saudi Arabia, Rabinowitz talked about a female teacher he met from that country and her reaction when asked about Saudi Arabia's ban on women driving. She did not oppose the ban and saw it as a symbol of respect and status. She thought women were so esteemed and respected that it was considered beneath them to drive. "We just don't see the world through the same lens. Who am I to judge how she feels?" Rabinowitz said to his students. He was the kind of teacher any child would be lucky to have, an educator who would never spoon-feed the answers. His approach mirrored the Wellesley Middle School philosophy: sixth graders should learn that there are many different perspectives.

Wellesley teachers spent as much time teaching about Christianity as Judaism and Islam, but while they took students to a mosque, a Jewish temple, and, on occasion, a Hindu temple, they did not visit a church. The assumption was that most students, Christian or not, had been inside a church. To give what they called an authentic experience in Christianity, teachers annually brought in a guest speaker. In early April 2011, as students finished their study of Christianity, more than three hundred filled the middle school auditorium to hear an associate professor of ministry studies at Harvard Divinity School. The speaker also was the choir director at Boston's Old South Church. The speaker sprinkled his speech with a PowerPoint presentation that began with a simple slide titled "The Christian Year." He tested students' knowledge about Christmas: "Do we know for a fact that Jesus was born on December 25?" "No," he and the students said in unison. Christians, he noted, chose that date, but no one really knows what day Jesus was born. In his talk, he made scant reference to spirituality.[25]

Wellesley's course, while it covered different religions' views on what happened after death, did not delve into spirituality. Teachers were coached to not be pro-religion and to also acknowledge that there were people who were not particularly religious. They did not teach a unit about atheists or agnostics, though, because they examined religion in the context of geography, history, and politics. Maybe that was a hole the teachers could eventually figure out how to fill, given that a growing number of Americans identify with no religion. The Divinity School professor's talk was in April, and usually students visited a mosque in May. School district and middle school administrators debated how to proceed and decided not to return to the Roxbury mosque. Instead, they chose the smaller mosque in Wayland, where no prayer service would be in progress and which no one had alleged had a link to terrorist groups.

—⁓—

In the aftermath of the backlash over the 2010 field trip, Rabinowitz began to question a few of his old practices. He used to love the idea of students seeing and experiencing a concept. As part of the Judaism unit, he picked a random student and showed him or her how to drape a tallit, the traditional Jewish prayer shawl, over the shoulders. Then, he showed the student how to strap tefillin—black boxes with words of the Torah inserted inside—onto an arm and the head, an act some Jews perform during morning prayers. The student stood in front of the class as Rabinowitz explained how Jews used those ritual items. But after the complaints about Wellesley taking its students to see active worship, he stopped that practice. He was not sure that having students try on a prayer shawl stepped over a line, but he did not want to risk a problem. He had learned just how hot the topic of religion could be for some parents and for the community at large, whereas before he'd thought only about what was happening inside the classroom. Now he worried more about how something could be perceived.[26]

Rabinowitz did not poll his students on which religion they might belong to, but he tried to make the classroom an environment where it was all right to be yourself and, he hoped, even enjoy learning. When students walked in, the thirty-eight-year-old teacher played a pop song through the computer speakers, then gave a one-question trivia quiz. One day he wanted to know which president was assassinated in Buffalo, New York. On another, he wanted to know where Babe Ruth was from. He tossed a lollipop to the winners. He was not shy about revealing a little of himself to his students. A photo from his wedding just the previous October was on his classroom computer screen saver. When he played the Jason Mraz song "I'm Yours" one day at the start of class, he mentioned that he had walked down the aisle to that song at his wedding. By the time he began teaching his students about religion that winter, he knew the class fairly well because he had taught them during the first part of the school year.

The twenty-five students in the class that I followed were a sampling of the growing religious diversity of America. While the majority were Christian, the class included students who were Muslim, Buddhist, Hindu, and atheist. Early on, during a lunch period, about fifteen of the students fielded my questions over pizza in a classroom. What did they know about their own and other religions? Were they okay about taking such a class? Views were mixed. A few students saw it as just another required class. Others came in eager to fill gaps in their knowledge, including their ignorance of the fact that Christianity was made up of several branches. Catholic students didn't always realize that Baptist classmates were Christian, and vice versa.

Some students brought heavy baggage with them. Long before middle school, they were picked on because they were members of a religious minority. Celia Golod had been teased for being a Jew ever since her family moved from a largely Jewish area in New Jersey to the mostly Christian town of Wellesley. At the time, Celia was in third grade. During that first year in a Wellesley school, a kid came up to her with a ruler to measure her nose. Celia hid in a corner afterward. In fifth grade, around Christmas time, she clashed with peers who wanted to know why she did not believe in Jesus. They kept trying to tell Celia that she was wrong. "I just told them, 'I'm sorry for what I believe in.' For a little bit, it made me want to be Christian just so I could be like everyone else."[27] I listened to Celia and I ached inside, remembering having the same fleeting thought after my family moved to a rural Ohio town from New York State when I was in the middle of fourth grade. There were no Jews in our school other than my brothers and me. When Rabinowitz taught about Judaism in the global beliefs course, Celia often felt uncomfortable because it was her religion he was talking about. Sitting at her kitchen counter finishing dinner during my visit to her home, Celia was pessimistic about what the class could achieve. "People who do tease people about [their religions] probably will never learn," she said.

Her parents, David and Lisa Golod, shook their heads in disagreement. Both lawyers, they saw the sixth-grade class on religions as something that could make a difference, even if their daughter did not see immediate effects. Religion aside, Celia was having a rough transition during her first year of middle school. She was, like all sixth graders, figuring out where she fit. Her parents thought her pessimism and skepticism could be a part of that angst.

"But maybe you're making a dent," Lisa Golod told her daughter. "Do you think, Celia, the fact that you understand more about Christianity makes you more understanding?"

Celia nodded. "Yeah," she said. "I didn't realize that Christianity came out of Judaism. Now we're all related." She crossed her fingers to indicate the connection.

All the way throughout the religions class, Rabinowitz nudged students to discern what was alike and different among the religions. Toward the end of the Christianity unit, he handed out worksheets with a Venn diagram. One circle was labeled "Judaism," the other "Christianity." The overlap was labeled "both." He gave students a worksheet of forty-four statements about the religions and urged them to work in groups. Celia and her classmates huddled at sets of four desks and loud chatter filled the room. "Believe that Jesus was Jewish." Students easily got that one. Both Jews and Christians believe that, they said. And they sorted out that baptism was a Christian ritual only. Another question about kneeling during services tripped up some students. "I don't kneel during services," said a girl who was Christian. But some Christians do, countered a boy who was Hindu. Maybe, the girl said, the answer was both for kneeling. Rabinowitz announced, "Twelve minutes, seven seconds to get all forty-four of these in the right place." Debates at the tables continued until the teacher said loudly, "One minute, twelve seconds." Then a few students clustered around him, begging for hints to the trickier statements. "I'm not telling you," the teacher said with a smile and shooed them away. "I want them to debate," he said to me in an aside. "The hard thing is kids want right versus wrong. There isn't always a right."

Midway through the course, Celia's parents saw their daughter gain more knowledge about her own religion. She had to give a PowerPoint presentation on Judaism to them and others as part of a class assignment and drew not only from her own experience in Hebrew school but from outside sources. Then she had to interview Christians as part of an assignment about Christianity. The class led the family to have more conversations at home about religion, particularly as the students began their study of Islam. As we sat around a table for four in their kitchen, the Golods got into the kind of discussion they had grown accustomed to since Celia started taking Rabinowitz's class. On a couch in the nearby sunken living room, Celia's younger brother, a third grader, did homework. Trixie the dog pawed at each of us, demanding attention. To the Golods, what the sixth graders were learning about Islam was the most critical part of the semester. "It's important," Lisa Golod said, "that they understand the good and bad. Religion sparks a lot of controversy. But there's good in all of them."

"My theory is there are terrorists in all religions," Celia said.

Her father, David Golod, jumped in: "You know what those terrorists are called? They're extremists."

Celia acknowledged that she used to think that all Muslims living outside of America were bad. The perfect world, she mused, would be one where there were no religions. Religion leads to too much strife.

"But wouldn't the world be boring without it?" her father asked. "She's looking at the negative side of religion. Religion is important because at the base of all religions is a sense of community and a sense of right and wrong. It's what humans do to instill ethics." It was as if Celia's parents were trying a case. On one side was their seemingly cynical daughter who had a hard time believing a class on religion would change how others treated her, treated other Jews, or treated anyone who was not Christian. On the other were a mother and father sure that Wellesley's religion course was a necessity that would make a difference.

—\~—

Zain Tirmizi, another student in Rabinowitz's class, is a Muslim boy who lives across the street from Jackson Posnik, one of the boys who joined the line of worshippers on the previous year's mosque field trip. The first time I met Zain, he expressed optimism about the class before more than a dozen of his peers: "Many people in America have stereotypes about Muslims. I'm glad they can teach it. I can say, 'I'm Muslim. I do this.' I'm very proud of it." At age twelve, he showed a quiet confidence, a confidence his parents had worked hard to build up in him, particularly in the aftermath of 9/11.

His parents, Ali and Hadia Tirmizi, almost didn't send Zain to the predominantly white Wellesley Middle School out of fear he would be bullied as one of the few Muslims. Zain has chestnut-colored skin, dark hair, and brown eyes. In his elementary school, he, as far as he knows, was the only Muslim. He remembered clearly the day he was taunted. In fourth grade, a boy approached Zain at his locker and said, "You're a Muslim. I'm going to check you for bombs." Zain told his father about the incident and Ali Tirmizi told him to correct the boy's stereotypes about Muslims. So Zain explained to the boy what his religion was. The pair eventually became good friends.[28] At a young age, Zain had the tools to educate his peers because his parents had grounded him well in his own religion. His parents, both physicians, immigrated to the United States in the late 1990s from Pakistan. Zain's family felt comfortable and included in their neighborhood. They lived in a two-story home toward the end of a cul-de-sac where Zain and his younger brother got invited to birthday parties featuring outside inflatable bounce houses and neighbors gathered for block parties. The Tirmizis felt accepted even though they were painfully aware that many Americans started viewing them as people to fear after Muslim terrorists flew airplanes into the World Trade Center towers.

"The first day I felt like an outsider in America was a day after 9/11," Hadia Tirmizi recalled as we spoke in the family's living room.

She was at her job in the hospital, walking in the corridors as she made patient rounds, and could not help but wonder if everyone was looking at her differently. No one picked on her. In fact, her colleagues came up to her to see if she were all right as anti-Muslim sentiment rose around the country and some Muslims were attacked.[29] Like her son, she had an air of confidence as she leaned back on her living room sofa and told me about the challenges of raising two Muslim boys in America. As Zain grew older, his parents fielded his questions about why people hated Muslims and about why a pastor in Florida would burn the Koran, a book the young boy had grown to treasure. On one of my visits to Zain's home, he took out his Koran and talked about how it was a gift from his grandmother. A few moments later, he brought out a little plate decorated with a verse from the Koran known as the Kursi prayer. He then chanted the prayer in Arabic. He recited the prayer, meant to ward off evil, every night over his younger brother because his brother was afraid of the dark. Incidents in which people burned or criticized the Koran make Zain sad. He talked to his parents about how he wished he could speak with those people and explain that the Koran was not something evil, and his mother offered consolation by saying that some people, like that pastor, were misguided. Maligners of Islam did not understand that his family was normal, with parents hoping for a good future for their children and a nice retirement for themselves.

Zain's home was a blend of his faith and of America. In the dining room, the family had a framed parchment of Arabic calligraphy by a renowned Pakistani calligrapher. The words were from the beginning of the Koran: "I start in the name of Allah, the beneficent, the merciful." On the wall, near the piece of calligraphy, was an image of the stamp of Mohammed. The house displayed souvenirs from their travels: a terra-cotta sculpture from France, a humpback whale made of clay from Cape Cod, and, on the door of Zain's room, a ski slope sign from Killington, Vermont. Zain also had a collection of coins from India, Pakistan, and Britain on his bedroom dresser near a *Star Wars* storm-trooper piggy bank.

Zain's parents emphasized to him that Muslim-haters were often just ignorant. Hadia Tirmizi did fear that her sons would become affected by such outspoken hatred in America toward Muslims, even though she believed her children would be fine in the Wellesley schools. She and her husband put heavy stock in the power of Wellesley's global beliefs course because the students repeatedly received the message that they should not lump every person of the same faith together, nor should they fear other religions. When Ali Tirmizi was growing up in Pakistan, where Muslims were in the majority, there was bias against India, heavily populated by Hindus. When he lived in India for five years, there was bias against Pakistan and the Muslims. Living in both countries, he grew to realize people essentially were the same and that there was no religion that advised its followers to kill, lie, rape, and plunder. One of his longtime friends was Hindu. Ali learned to accept others through exposure, and he thinks the sixth graders will do the same through education. When Zain's sixth-grade class studied Islam, his parents visited as guest speakers one day on a break from work. His mother's long, wavy brown hair hung loose around her shoulders. She wore a hijab only inside mosques. She and her husband were not trained scholars on Islam, and both stressed that they were talking about Islam only from their own perspective. Zain's mother described the pillars of Islam, including the obligation to pray five times a day, but admitted she simply could not find time for all five prayers in her day as a mother of two and a physician. She and her husband gave students a very human look at their religion.

When Rabinowitz began the unit on Islam, he first drilled students on the basics. They learned definitions and came to know that "Islam" was the word that referred to the religion, while "Muslim" denoted a follower of Islam. Then Rabinowitz asked them to give common stereotypes of Muslims, and the students gave a familiar list: "All Muslims are terrorists." "All Muslim women are oppressed." "All Muslims are Arabs." He took each of those stereotypes and worked to dispel them, using a world map to show where

Muslims lived. The country with the biggest population was Indonesia, that fact that stumped so many Americans in a national poll.

"As we said yesterday, do most Muslims in the world live in the Middle East?" he asked the class.

"No," the students shouted.

As the unit progressed, they watched a television news clip about Muslims' push to include their major holidays on New York City's school vacation calendar. In the video, a Muslim speaker said that 12 percent of the city's public school students are Muslim so the school system should recognize their holidays. The mayor, though, countered that there were not enough school days in the calendar to accommodate every religion's holiday. The teachers union backed the Muslims' wishes. Rabinowitz wanted the students to debate whether Wellesley should have Muslim holidays off.

"I know it's very easy for you to say, 'Of course, they should have their holidays off,'" the teacher said, but he pushed them to think of all sides. One girl thought the school district should give at least one day off for Muslim holidays. "What's the big deal?" she wondered. Around her, some students disagreed. Then the school year would need to be extended, and school already did not end until late June. "Think of this school where the Muslim population is not high. Would it matter for them?" the teacher asked. Zain made the case that both Muslim and Hindu holidays were neglected on the school calendar. He took days off during Ramadan, then played catch-up on homework. Because of the religious observance, he could not do homework until the evening, when the fasting period ended. Anand Ghorpadey, a student in the class, brought Zain his homework, but Anand did not agree that the schools should change the calendar for Muslims or for Hindus, who were so few. Anand, a self-described atheist who celebrated Hindu holidays with his family, said students had the right to stay home from school and not do homework on their holidays.

After the class ended, Zain and Anand continued the debate as they walked into the hall toward their next class. "I want my education. It's hard to catch up," Zain said, adding that he also wanted to be able to celebrate the Muslim holidays with his family. Anand raised his eyebrows. "Hard to catch up three days, Zain?" His friend was insistent: "We should have both Hindu and Muslim holidays off." Anand grinned and shook his head. "None." The pair, friends since kindergarten, agreed to disagree.

In early May, as the class began preparing for the field trip to the Wayland mosque, Zain told me that he was wondering whether the teachers could cover Islam just as well without visiting a mosque. While many of his classmates were excited, he was not. He thought they had high expectations because of slides Rabinowitz had shown of famous mosques, palatial structures with minarets and domes. His mosque was small with no dome or minaret. He was not ashamed of it but wasn't sure what it would accomplish to tour there. Many of his other classmates were excited and a little nervous. One girl had seen the outside of the Wayland mosque before and was enthusiastic about seeing the inside, but worried about wearing the wrong thing because she knew there was a dress code. The school asked students to keep shoulders covered and dress fairly modestly.

In class before the May 9, 2011, field trip, a year after the Roxbury mosque tour, Rabinowitz reviewed what students already knew, including the differences between Sunni and Shi'a Muslims. The Shi'a believe that only kin of the prophet Mohammed should have become leaders of the religion after him, while Sunnis thought the most qualified person, regardless of lineage, should have. After the review, the teacher walked around the classroom handing out worksheets titled "Exploring Mosques Around the World" and announced, "You are all reporters sent out on this voyage. Look at at least twenty mosques around the world. There are no right or wrong answers. Explore, explore, explore." The students used provided laptops and worked cooperatively to identify mosques with the most beautiful minarets; the biggest, smallest, or most beautiful domes; and the greatest use of color. Rabinowitz used the exercise to give students a sense of the diversity among mosques and within one faith.

Zain worked with Timmy Yee. Because he identified with no particular religion and knew little about any faith, Timmy saw the class as particularly important for him. He thought he should know something about religions even if he did not believe in any of them. "Whoa, this is awesome," he said to Zain. "Dude, look at the Prophet's Mosque in Medina." The Prophet's Mosque, in Saudi Arabia, also known as the Al-Masjid al-Nabawi, had twenty-four domes and could hold up to 500,000 worshippers.[30] Zain looked. "I feel sorry for my mosque," he said. "It's so small." The Wayland mosque served 350 to 400 families. As Zain and Timmy huddled, Rabinowitz walked over and asked Zain, "If I play the call to prayer, is that offensive?" Zain shook his head no. "Why would that be offensive?" he said. "It's okay." As the call to prayer came in over the classroom computer speakers, the teacher talked over it: "This is the call to prayer you'd hear from a minaret. When I was in Jordan, I'd hear this all the time." Then he quieted, letting students hear the Arabic chant as they worked.

The next day, when they toured the Wayland mosque, the students would not hear the call to prayer because the school intentionally planned to be there when there was no chance of active worship. Rabinowitz, in his usual work attire of button-down shirt and khaki pants, peered at students through his wire rim glasses as they sat on the yellow bus outside the school parking lot, ready to head out to Wayland. "Remember, the reason we're going to the mosque is to continue our learning," he said in a voice just a tad stern. He held up a hand to quell the chatter and giggles from the already fidgety eleven- and twelve-year-olds. "I want to be proud of your behavior. Make us proud in how you ask questions."

I sat next to Katie Pyzowski, who picked a window seat. Katie, who sang in her Episcopal youth church choir, had traveled extensively with her family and visited churches and even a monastery in Greece.

She had felt like she was intruding on the holy places. When her family stopped by a monastery in the Greek countryside, Katie at first wanted to stay in the car. A few days before when I chatted with her at her home, she was conflicted about seeing the mosque. On the bus ride, though, Katie was more excited than nervous. In just fifteen minutes or so, after passing a stretch of two-story homes with manicured lawns, we reached a small business strip and the bus pulled into the parking lot of the Islamic Center of Boston in Wayland. It was a rectangular building that could pass for offices if not for a few touches of Middle Eastern architecture, including triangular, trellis-like arches. No dome. No minaret, just as Zain had described.

As students poured out of the buses and lined up behind teachers, three women in hijabs waited outside. They were volunteer tour guides, led by Sepi Gilani, the mosque's vice president and a surgeon. Gilani also is a parent of eighteen-year-old twins who went to a nearby public school system and studied world religions as part of a seventh-grade world history course. They spent a month on each religion they studied but did not go on field trips. In Gilani's view, tours would be a plus. As she faced the 150 sixth graders from Wellesley, she worked hard to keep them interested. "This tour is going to be like one at an amusement park," she announced. At 20,000 square feet, the Wayland building was less than a third the size of the Roxbury mosque. The students followed Gilani up a set of stairs, where volunteers told them about each room, including a library and classrooms where Zain had attended religious school. They came back downstairs, and at their guide's urging, looked inside the bathrooms to see the washing stations Muslims use before prayer. Outside the prayer hall, they followed instructions to remove their shoes. They went inside the hall and sat in rows on the green-and-gold rug. Gilani began a half-hour PowerPoint presentation about the beliefs and practices of Islam. "Asalmu-aleikum," the first slide said in phonetic Arabic, or "Peace be with you." She gave a primer on the Islamic world's view on creation, then moved on to the meaning of the word Islam itself: "submission," which means submitting to God's rule. She revealed a little about herself, talking about how she grew up in Kansas City with her parents, who were born in Iran. She described her trip to Mecca as a slide appeared of her and her family dressed in white on their pilgrimage. Then she fielded questions.

One student wanted to know why they had to take off their shoes to enter the worship space. Gilani cited a practical reason: "We pray with our foreheads on the ground. If we kept our shoes on, we'd get our heads all dirty. It's to keep them clean."

Another student asked why the tour guide wore a hijab. Gilani said it was an obligation to wear a head covering, though she wore it only inside the mosque. At work, in her daily life, her hair showed. She referred to another woman standing in the back, who wore the hijab all the time, and asked her to talk about her practice. The woman was the same person who had led the Roxbury mosque field trip the year before. "For me, not displaying a woman's beauty in public is about modesty," she told the students. "It's empowering not to be judged on the basis of physical appearance but rather on the basis of one's deeds." Later, she told me that Wellesley's decision not to return to her mosque in Roxbury saddened her. She was the tour leader and knew the rules about separation of church and state. What had happened in Roxbury was out of the ordinary on tours at the mosque. Wellesley, in her view, caved into the very Islamophobia the sixth graders learned about when they watched a CNN documentary about community opposition to mosque construction in Murfreesboro, Tennessee. That video showed the students how Muslims were demonized and generalized. That was what happened to the Roxbury mosque when the video came out about the 2010 field trip. Why not, she asked, bring Wellesley students back to Roxbury to show that the school system knew the mosque was not trying to convert its students?[31]

For Wellesley teachers and administrators, it was too risky a venture. They did not want to provoke the group that had opposed the trip and bring more unwanted attention to the school. Some parents accompanied the students on the Wayland trip, but there were no secret videos shot this time. Afterward, students praised the roughly hour-long tour and many told me they figured it would be the only time they would get to see a mosque. Zain left with a sense of pride, liking that the tour demystified aspects of Islam for his peers, including the part about why Muslims take shoes off for prayer. Seeing the mosque had fascinated Katie. The sense that she was intruding faded once she was inside the mosque, where she saw the expansive worship space and the mihrab she had only seen pictures of before. She understood what Wellesley was trying to do with the global beliefs class. The key word, she said, was "about." Rabinowitz was not teaching her how to be Muslim, Jewish, Hindu, or Christian. He was not trying to make her do something. He was simply teaching her about different religions.[32]

Rabinowitz's teaching style helped many students feel comfortable speaking about religion, a topic so many adults prefer to avoid. That morning icebreaker of playing pop songs particularly made an impression on Celia, the girl who had doubts about what the class could accomplish. The last day of the school year, she presented the teacher with a CD collection of songs, including his favorite, Mraz's "I'm Yours." During the refrain, the teacher nudged every sixth grader in the room to sing along with him. "Doo, doo, whoa whoa," they sang, and their teacher coaxed them: "Nice and loud." It could have been an awkward moment. These were preteens, after all. But Rabinowitz's natural affability and touch of goofiness made it work and cracked some of that barrier between youth and adult. I couldn't help but contrast his version of an icebreaker with what a math teacher of mine did when I was in eighth grade. He told Polish jokes.

In 2013, I circled back to Celia, Zain, and Katie and met with them in their homes. Celia, jaded as an eleven-year-old, now seemed like a wiser thirteen-year-old. She did not view the course as a panacea for bullying or teasing but thought it made a difference. As she moved through the middle school grades, she experienced less ribbing because of her religion. The defining moment? In some ways, it was her October 2012 bat mitzvah ceremony at Temple Beth Elohim. Roughly eighty of her peers attended and many came from her middle school. She was amazed to see how excited her school friends were to attend her bat mitzvah and not just because of the party after the service. Having heard about this coming-of-age ritual in the world religions course, they liked the idea of seeing it in person. Celia thinks she grew more positive about the course's ability to change attitudes partly because she matured. As a sixth grader, she was quick to judge everyone and their treatment of her. In an eighth-grade class about world foods, students brought in foods that represented their cultures. Celia helped her mother make matzo ball soup. When Celia brought it in, students were excited and said, "Oh, you eat this on Passover, right?" The girl who used to feel like the odd one out felt special in that moment. "Did it make you feel prouder to be Jewish?" I asked. "Yeah," Celia answered as she finished frosting a cake she had baked for a retiring homeroom teacher.[33] The course also made her feel less ignorant about several religions, particularly Islam, which previously had seemed so foreign. She remembered the holidays of different religions.

For Katie, some of the details about the various religions did not stick. I asked if she remembered what Ramadan was. It was the first week of July 2013 and the holiday had just started. Katie shook her head. She had forgotten that one. What did stick? She kept what she called an awareness of other religions' beliefs and thought she could hold her own if she met someone of a different faith and they started to talk about their religion. She suspected some of the lessons would come back, whether it was about a holiday, a religious figure, or beliefs.

Zain, like Katie, also forgot some of the course content. He started trying on his own to learn more about religions, especially polytheistic ones like Hinduism. Other than the information he gained, he experienced intangible benefits from the class, particularly in the aftermath of the 2013 Boston Marathon bombings. The suspects were a pair of brothers, the Tsarnaevs, originally from Chechnya, and to Zain and his parents' dismay, they soon were identified as Muslims who had gone radical. Not long after the bombings, which killed three and injured several hundred others near the marathon finish line, Zain had a substitute teacher in his eighth-grade social studies class. She began talking about how certain Muslims were coming into the country, taking the nation's resources, and then doing things like the marathon bombings. Several of Zain's classmates looked over at him, trying to see if he was upset. Zain was about to speak up in protest when the teacher retracted her statement and said, "I don't mean all Muslims." The next day, the class spoke about the incident with their regular teacher. If it were not for the sixth-grade world religions course, Zain doubts that many of his peers would have thought the substitute teacher had done anything wrong. He believes the course made students more willing to speak up if they thought a religion was wrongly stereotyped.

The same summer I revisited Zain, Celia, and Katie, I sat down with four Wellesley High School students about to start their senior year. Nearly six years after taking the class, all agreed that their memories of what they learned were fuzzy. "Okay, what's Ramadan? Does anyone know?" I asked as we sat around a kitchen table in one of the student's homes. "No," two of them said and laughed in embarrassment. A third, Aidan Cort, who is Catholic and a peer minister at his church, guessed that Ramadan related to Judaism. The fourth student, Cecilia Milano, who grew up Unitarian and now attends the congregational church in the main village square, said she was sure it was the Muslim fasting period. Right answer.[34] "Okay, Koran, does anyone know?" I said, continuing an ultrabrief quiz. This time, they answered in unison: "The holy book of Islam."

All of them, no matter how much they remembered, said the course's most important lesson was teaching them to respect other religions. Not to mention, the course, unlike many of the other classes, was relevant to their lives. Cecilia, who had an internship that summer with a state representative, thought she became less judgmental because of the class. When she walked from South Station, a subway train stop, to the State House, she saw Muslim women wearing hijabs. She knew that it was a part of their culture, their religion. It was how they practiced their religion, nothing more. In the past, she might have looked askance at someone wearing a head covering. Their classes took field trips, but only to Temple Beth Elohim. Just seeing a Jewish temple left an impact. Aidan felt better prepared when he attended a friend's bar or bat mitzvah. He remembered he was pleased that he understood something about the temple's customs, including simply knowing what a yarmulke was and that wearing it did not mean he was converting to Judaism. Before the course, he thought that the synagogue would frown upon his wearing it because he was not Jewish. His experience was with his Catholic church, which allows only Catholics to perform certain rituals, such as taking communion. In this boy, and in so many others I spoke with, the wish of the Wellesley social studies chair was coming true. These teens were more comfortable around other faiths than many of their parents had been as children.

But Wellesley teachers, scarred by that infamous tour of the Roxbury mosque, became more careful with how they conducted the classes and field trips. They avoided anything that looked like students were participating in a ritual act, including putting on religious garb. No longer would Wellesley take students on a field trip to a house of worship where there was active prayer. But teachers could not control what tour guides might do. On a spring 2013 field trip to Temple Beth Elohim, about two hundred students exited school buses onto the sidewalks of the temple, housed in a three-year-old, 42,000-square-foot building, a complex that gave visitors a sense that they were seeing a bit of Israel. The pale yellowish stone walls were made of Jerusalem stone, named so because they resembled the construction commonly seen in Jerusalem's Old City. The temple's associate rabbi, a woman in her early thirties, beckoned students and teachers to follow her into the sanctuary.

As each student walked by, the rabbi handed out a black yarmulke, also known as a *kippah*. One of the teachers winced at the sight and spoke softly with Rabinowitz about what to do. The mosque controversy was in the backs of their minds. A few students appeared to be making fun of the small black caps, but teachers had a bigger concern. By asking students to cover their heads, were they engaging in a ritual act? The teachers had not encountered this on past field trips to the temple.

The associate rabbi, who wore a yarmulke, stepped to the front and faced the students sitting in rows of seats, ready to give a talk about Judaism and the worship space itself. Before the rabbi could speak, a female teacher walked over and whispered in her ear about the concerns over the yarmulkes. The teacher then stood in front of the students and announced, "I'm going to ask people who are wearing the *kippahs*, if you are Jewish, you can wear them. If not, take them off." The majority of the students took them off.

CHAPTER THREE

Whose Truth Should They Hear?

EVERY TIME Hassan Shibly lectures about his Muslim faith at schools, he takes listeners back to his childhood and Chuck E. Cheese's. He was a young boy eating at the restaurant with his father when the time for Muslim evening prayer arrived, and his father did what he would have done anywhere. He stood, bowed, and began praying in Arabic. The restaurant manager walked over, bowed too, and asked, "Is the floor dirty? Is there something wrong there?"

Shibly's father said nothing. He moved into the next stage of prayer, knelt, and leaned his forehead against the floor likely coated with pizza crumbs. "Sir, does the floor stink?" the manager asked as he bent down to look. Again, Shibly's father did not respond, though the manager obviously had good intentions. An observant Muslim, Shibly's father would never break during prayer.

Seven times on November 29, 2011, Shibly told that Chuck E. Cheese's story to world history and world religions classes at Steinbrenner High, a sprawling stucco-like building with a grassy quadrangle and palm trees near a pond in Lutz, Florida, a Tampa suburb. Shibly was a guest speaker, invited to give nearly five hundred students a talk about Islam to complement their studies. When he stood before each class, Shibly, then twenty-five, wore a kufi, a rounded cap many Muslims wear, and kept his curly brown beard at fist length to pay homage to a custom set by the prophet Mohammed. Shibly, now a lawyer and imam, used the Chuck E. Cheese's anecdote to preface a lesson about the articles of faith in Islam, including the obligation to pray five times a day. "We're about to learn the articles of faith. It's important so you don't end up like the guy at Chuck E. Cheese," Shibly told the students. He and his father knew that the restaurant manager was not trying to be rude and that he just did not understand that he was seeing a Muslim in the act of prayer. Shibly delivered a PowerPoint presentation on Islam at Steinbrenner High, but it was that Chuck E. Cheese's anecdote that many teens remembered most. He gave the students a sense of what ignorance looks like. And he gave Islam a human face.[1]

Less than a month later, just the fact that the twentysomething Muslim had set foot in a public high school in Tampa caused outrage. No one talked about the way Shibly engaged history students. Shibly and the teacher who invited him, Kelly Miliziano, became targets of anti-Muslim and conservative activists. Much of the ire was directed at the group Shibly headed, the Florida chapter of CAIR, the Council on American-Islamic Relations, a Muslim civil rights organization that had been accused by various bloggers of having ties to terrorist groups. His appearance as a guest speaker stoked debate about whose truth was okay for children to hear when the topic was religion.

Born in Syria, Shibly moved to a suburb of Buffalo, New York, at age four with his parents, both dentists who taught at the State University of New York at Buffalo. In high school, he started speaking about Islam to students at his world history teacher's invitation. He became a regular guest lecturer in world history classes in suburban Buffalo high schools for the next several years while he earned an undergraduate degree and then a law degree at SUNY Buffalo.

Shibly wasn't surprised by the venom that surfaced after his visits to Steinbrenner were publicized. He had been through it all before.

He came from a family with activist roots and made headlines before he finished college. In 2004, after attending a religion conference on Islam in Toronto, he and his mother were among several dozen Muslims held for six hours, photographed, and fingerprinted after they crossed the border from Canada back into the United States. Shibly and his mother, along with three other Muslim Americans who were detained, sued the government, charging harassment. A federal judge dismissed the suit, saying he could not tell Homeland Security not to conduct such inspections.[2] Shibly, just a freshman in college, was featured in a positive article in his college paper about his and his mother's fight for rights for Muslims. But as a nineteen-year-old college junior, Shibly made comments that anti-Islam groups resurrected many times to paint him as a supporter of terrorists. The summer of 2006, Shibly visited Syria to see relatives as Israel's conflict with Lebanon escalated. When he returned, he spoke to his college magazine about the devastation he saw as Lebanese refugees came into Syria. The teenage Shibly described Hezbollah as "a resistance movement supported in Lebanon, by both Muslims and Christians. It is not merely a military institution; it provides a lot of social services for people of all different faiths. They're absolutely not a terrorist organization; their targets have always been military targets."[3]

Those words he said as a nineteen-year-old haunted him in 2010 after he spoke at Clarence High School in suburban Buffalo; a year later, when he was hired to lead CAIR in Tampa; and after his Steinbrenner visits. He had spoken at Clarence about Islam several times without incident, but in the spring of 2010 a parent raised concerns, saying her son had heard Shibly contend that the 9/11 attackers were not Muslims but atheists and that the attacks happened because of American's blind support for Israel. A pro-Israel group and a conservative radio talk show host joined the fray and built up opposition against Shibly, then a law student, and used his old comments about Hezbollah as ammunition. Both the school's principal and teachers said they did not believe Shibly's statements were inflammatory.[4] Shibly said he had been trying to make the point that the 9/11 terrorists were not motivated by Islam or religion and that they did not represent the faith he held so dear.[5]

In response to the furor over Shibly's talk, Clarence school board members decided to tighten a controversial-issues policy that had few specifics other than requiring teachers to get a principal's approval before bringing in a speaker on a controversial topic. The superintendent and school board now had to be informed about a scheduled presentation involving controversial issues thirty days before the event and parents had to be notified at least five days ahead of time. Parents could have their children excused from the presentation by sending a written note to the principal. But what was a "controversial" issue? The policy left that decision to the superintendent.[6] The Clarence board's actions disappointed Shibly, and he hoped for more from the Hillsborough County School Board in Tampa.

Clarence, 94 percent white with a smattering of minority groups, was a town of just 30,000 that had previously tried to ban Harry Potter books. Tampa, almost one hundred times the size of Clarence, was much more diverse but with a heavy conservative influence. The region, and Florida as a whole, was a magnet for high-profile anti-Muslim sentiment. The preacher who carried out his threat to burn Korans in 2010 was from Gainesville and later moved to the Tampa area. A small group of state lawmakers repeatedly tried to pass a measure to ban the practice of foreign law in the state, a bill that sponsors said was an attempt to stop the use of sharia law, the Muslim religious law based on the Koran. Leading the campaign for the bill was David Caton, the Tampa-based head of the Florida Family Council who had successfully persuaded the multibillion-dollar retailer Lowe's to remove its advertisements from a new national cable reality television show about American Muslim families. Caton, who had gotten supporters to send thousands of e-mails to Tampa school board members to protest removing Good Friday as a school holiday, later used the same tactic to oppose Shibly's Steinbrenner appearance.

Shibly had tried to clear the air regarding his past statements about Hezbollah. Shortly after his hiring as head of CAIR-Florida, he wrote a message on his website to critics upset about what he had once said about Hezbollah.[7] Today, given what he knows, Shibly says he would have no problem calling Hezbollah a terrorist organization. He said he had made those remarks because he wanted to emphasize the reality of the political landscape in Lebanon and make the point that Israel's bombing of that country in the 2006 conflict could not be justified by international standards. Shibly noted how his detractors blew his words out of proportion to make him look like a radical. Part of his current job at CAIR-Florida was to educate the public about Islam and dispel stereotypes of Muslims.

For years, Miliziano, the chair of Steinbrenner's history department, and her colleagues had invited a variety of guest speakers, including Muslim clergy, a Buddhist monk, and a rabbi, to add to lessons about world religions. Miliziano had invited Shibly at a local imam's recommendation. Though he had only come to Tampa in June 2011 to head CAIR, Shibly already had established a reputation in the Tampa Bay interfaith community as an articulate spokesman for his faith. As an imam, he also gave sermons at area mosques. Steinbrenner teachers took special care to find Muslim guest speakers because Islam was the religion most of their students knew the least about. The roughly 200,000-student Hillsborough County school system overall was diverse: the majority of students were either Hispanic, Asian, black, or a mix of races, while 38 percent were white. Steinbrenner was more homogeneous and predominantly white, with roughly a third of its students from other racial or ethnic groups.[8] Faculty and students at Steinbrenner say Christianity was the dominant religion at the school, which is based in Lutz, a high-income suburb dotted with horse farms, gated communities, and country clubs. The nearby evangelical Christian megachurch, Idlewild, drew many members from among Steinbrenner's 2,250 students and provided speakers for Christian club meetings at the high school. The principal was firm in her belief that no clergy should roam the cafeteria during lunch hour and had shooed away youth pastors.

Miliziano, who has a doctorate in global education, had taught for nearly a quarter of a century, including eight years at an American school in Greece. She had traveled to the Middle East and seen houses of worship of multiple religions, including mosques, but as a Catholic, the teacher believed a Muslim would bring a perspective she could not give.[9] It took me months to get Miliziano's permission to meet with her in Tampa and see her classes. She worried about too much disruption at a school that had already been through so much. She, too, had been hurt by it all. The teacher did not know that anyone had an issue with Shibly's visit until about a week later, when her supervisor received a complaint from a student's father. The father, a land development consultant in his late forties, became worried about the guest speaker's appearance after his daughter mentioned that her class had had a guest talk about Islam.[10] Michael Johnson (the name is a pseudonym by his request) asked if the speaker was an imam, and his daughter said he was someone from an organization but that she didn't remember the name. Johnson asked what the speaker had talked about. "Just about Islam," said his daughter, who was not bothered by anything the speaker had said.

But Johnson, a Lutheran who described himself as a conservative libertarian, was concerned. He wanted to know which organization the speaker represented. He was suspicious that it could be CAIR, which he saw as a group with a checkered past. He had read about CAIR urging members not to cooperate with the FBI. A few days later, he had his concerns affirmed when he read a post by Pamela Geller on her blog, *Atlas Shrugs*. The headline for the December 4, 2011, post read "Child Abuse: Hamas-Linked CAIR Poisoning Minds of High School Students." The Southern Poverty Law Center, a civil rights group, described Geller, an author of a book about the "Islamization of America," as the anti-Muslim movement's "most visible and flamboyant figurehead."[11] In her first post about the school talks, Geller reported on CAIR's seven presentations to a high school but didn't name Steinbrenner. In her opening salvo, she wrote, "Hamas-linked groups are talking to high school students? Co-conspirators in the largest terror funding trial in our nation's history? Is that what our public schools are doing with our children—subjecting them to indoctrination and propaganda? That is child abuse. Where are the counter voices? Where are the voices of freedom?"[12] Reading those words, Johnson became increasingly alarmed. The next day, he went to Steinbrenner to voice his concerns about the guest speaker and met with Kelly King, an assistant principal and Miliziano's supervisor at the time.

Johnson, who emphasized that he had no problem with the school teaching about Islam, wanted the administrator to agree not to have CAIR speakers at Steinbrenner.[13] In that meeting and in a later joint call with King and the teacher, Johnson questioned whether the school had done its research on CAIR and the speaker. Johnson, when he found out the speaker was Hassan Shibly, did a Google search on Shibly's name and immediately saw that he was listed as refusing to consider Hamas and Hezbollah as terrorist organizations. He told the teacher she didn't know the dangers she had led her students into. Miliziano chafed. "Yes, I do, sir," she responded, and added, "I think you need to check your sources, sir, because that sounds like Islamophobic jargon."

I could picture the plucky fifty-three-year-old teacher saying those words. Around five feet, five inches tall, Miliziano, who oversaw her department, had a confident professional demeanor. She also showed a passion for standing up for the underdog. As students walked into her classroom, they saw a framed poster of a famous quotation by Martin Niemöller, a Lutheran pastor who spoke out against the Nazis during World War II and spent seven years in concentration camps. *"First they came for the Communists, but I was not a Communist so I did not speak out,"* the quotation starts.

". . . They came for the Jews and I did not speak out because I was not a Jew. Then they came for me—and there was no one left to speak for me."[14] The teacher displayed the poster to make students think about what they would do if they saw someone being persecuted.

In Johnson's view, the teacher and her supervisor had discounted him as anti-Muslim and ignored a legitimate issue: which types of speakers should be allowed to speak to students. If schools bring in speakers on religion, then they should make sure the guests have unblemished integrity, he said.[15] It bothered him, he said, that grassroots Muslims had not denounced Islamic terrorists (though, in fact, many, including leaders of CAIR chapters across the country, had). He believed, too, that Muslims in some states had made strong efforts to promote sharia law and he feared what could happen in this country because of Muslims' influence. None of that, he said, made him anti-Muslim. He asked me not to use his name because he didn't want his daughter to be teased. Calm and articulate in person, he raised a valid question: should schools avoid inviting speakers or organizations that have weathered controversy?

Johnson's complaint initially stayed at the school level, but Geller, who was based in the New York City area and had more than forty thousand followers on Twitter, stirred things up more on December 19, 2011, with an article on the *American Thinker* website headlined "Hamas High School in Florida?" This time, she identified Steinbrenner and wrote that "an informed source tells me it was the notorious Hassan Shibly" who spoke to the classes.[16]

Shibly called Miliziano after the article went viral. "It's out there now and you're going to get some ugliness toward you. We're used to it; you may not be," he warned the teacher.[17]

Founded in 1994, CAIR, the national parent organization of CAIR-Florida, had been in the news many times because of battles with the US Department of Justice over its characterization of the council. The Justice Department named CAIR as an unindicted coconspirator in a trial of the Holy Land Foundation for Relief and Development, a Texas-based charity accused of funneling millions of dollars in donations to Hamas. The government shut down Holy Land in 2001, and a federal judge later ruled that the foundation had financed Hamas and thus supported terrorism. CAIR and the national association of defense lawyers fought against the label "un-indicted co-conspirator" given to the Muslim civil rights group, one of more than three hundred organizations and individuals given the same designation in association with the Holy Land trial.[18] CAIR, like most of the groups, was never convicted of anything.

It had long been guilt by association, said Shibly, who leads CAIR-Florida's eleven employees out of two brick buildings near a commercial shopping strip. The group represents clients, mostly Muslims, in a variety of discrimination cases and also helps school children deal with bullying related to their religion. When Shibly and I first met, he acted as tour guide and teacher. He encouraged me to call him Hassan, but did not shake my hand and explained why. It was part of his faith not to touch or shake hands with a woman not related by blood. I knew of that practice among ob-servant Muslims and in many Orthodox Jewish sects. Shibly saw it as saving himself for his wife. He introduced me to his staff and made a point to note that his employees included Muslims and non-Muslims. The tour ended in his office, adorned with a few pic-tures, one of a verse from the Koran and one of the Seven Advices of Rumi, a thirteenth-century Sufi philosopher and poet. Rumi's words, to Shibly, represented part of Islam—a faith about peace. "In generosity and helping others, be like a river," Rumi's words of wisdom begin. "In compassion and grace, be like the sun." So ap-propriate to the firestorm encircling Shibly was this line: "In toler-ance, be like a sea." He had a personal stake in the outcome of the uproar over his Steinbrenner visit. He and his wife planned to raise their children in Hillsborough County and hoped to send them to the public schools. By 2014, the couple had three children, ages four, two, and one.

Minutes after Shibly called Miliziano to warn her of what she might face, the teacher heard "Bing, bing, bing," marking the arrival of multiple e-mails on her office computer. In e-mails at times laced with profanity, strangers told her she should be fired for letting a terrorist come speak to her students. Voice mails followed, and Miliziano kept three of the most abhorrent as reminders of the ignorance and hate that others spewed at her. "I have a PhD, too. Actually I have two PhDs," one caller said. "You are the scum of the earth and you do not represent women or any women in the United States, and you've never been in a Muslim stronghold . . . or you would not bring those filthy, stinky people into our schools to indoctrinate our little children." Miliziano felt numb and at a loss to understand the anger. Four other teachers had heard the same speaker. So had more than five hundred students. Shibly had not even mentioned sharia law.

Then a bad situation grew worse. Johnson, upset by the school's refusal to do anything about his complaint, wrote to the blogger, Geller, and gave his account of what had happened. In early January, Geller ran another blog post headlined "Hamas-Linked CAIR in Your Kid's Classroom: A Parent's First-Hand Account." The blogger incited her readers to "work the phones, demand equal time and a cease and desist from inviting Muslim Brotherhood groups to speak to public school students. Call for Ms. Miliziano's removal. Demand equal time for freedom fighters."[19] She also posted work e-mail addresses and phone numbers for Miliziano and for Steinbrenner's principal.

Early in January 2012, the controversy followed Miliziano home. "If you think your principal is going to be able to protect you, you're wrong," a man's voice said when Miliziano answered the phone. "We're going to get you one way or the other. You're not going to be allowed in the classroom. I'm going to do everything to make sure you're not in the classroom."

The teacher, who was home with her husband and their two children, then ages eight and eleven, responded in disbelief to the caller, "Do you realize you're calling me in my home at nine thirty tonight? Who are you?"

The man's answer frightened her. "You know who I am," he said.[20]

Miliziano filled out a police report, but nothing came of it. She struggled to understand the hostility directed her way. People claimed the teacher was trying to bring down the US government. Caton, of the Florida Family Council, submitted a Freedom of Information request for all of the teacher's e-mails with Shibly, and those e-mails, exchanges about the logistics of the visits, were widely circulated. Caton had the more national name, but it was Terry Kemple, the former executive director of the Christian Coalition of Florida, who became the main face of the opposition to Shibly's visit. Kemple lived in Brandon, a rural part of the county that was home to the region's other evangelical Christian powerhouse, the Bell Shoals Baptist Church, which had several thousand members. A member of Bell Shoals, Kemple ran a group that began in the church, the Community Issues Council, and used his organization to promote a variety of his stances. He opposed same-sex marriage and worked on a statewide effort to persuade voters to pass Amendment 2, which defined marriage as a union between a man and woman. When the CAIR speaker issue surfaced, he had run for the school board once, lost, and was about to run for a second time. He would lose that bid, too. Kemple created a website for his campaign against CAIR and a packet of literature to go inside a folder. Stapled to the outside was a flyer headlined "Parents Say NO to HAMAS! In Our Schools." At the bottom of the flyer, Kemple put a photo of Shibly in front of CAIR headquarters and wrote that "Hassan Shibly = CAIR, co-conspirator in the largest terror funding case in US History = HAMAS."

Kemple wore his conservatism on his sleeves, his cars, and around his home. He greeted me in an American flag shirt and blue jeans when I met him at his home. An American flag covered the back wall of his office, and on a living room table near the open Bible he said he read from daily were coasters with elephants and the motto "Republican, Conservative and Proud of It."[21] The sixty-seven-year-old father of three, who was also a grandfather and great-grandfather, was frank about his conservatism and about having found Jesus after years of living life on the wild side. Born in California, he moved around a lot as a child because his father was in the Navy. His troubles began at age thirteen when he started drinking. By the time he was in high school, he was a full-blown alcoholic. During his mid- to late twenties, he became a pot-smoking hippie with long hair and long beard, says Kemple, now balding with short gray hair. A college dropout, he fashioned a career in sales and marketing, and in the early 1980s moved to Florida and started a computer business with a friend. But alcoholism tore apart his first marriage and estranged him from his children. At age thirty-nine, after going to a revival at his older brother's church, he made a decision to accept Jesus Christ as his lord and savior.

He seemed amused by his notoriety in the Tampa Bay area, where a newspaper columnist has dubbed him "our fair hamlet's Good Book political huckster."[22] He acted out with relish the way a Hillsborough County commissioner had reacted to his request to be named to a countywide diversity council as a conservative voice. The commissioner stood on the dais, pointed his finger, and yelled at him, "Mr. Kemple hates gays," recalled Kemple, who rose from his leather couch, pointing his finger and mimicking the commissioner's shrill tone.

Kemple, after consulting a Jacksonville man who led a group fighting radical Islam, created an education coalition to oppose CAIR speakers in schools. Asked his views on Islam, Kemple referred me to a blue folder with the flyer. He said he was concerned that CAIR had been linked to the funding of terrorism. He acknowledged he was no expert on the subject so had sought others' wisdom before he made his case against Steinbrenner. He took the conversation in another direction when asked about schools teaching about world religions. He wanted to emphasize that he believed America was founded primarily by Christians and on Christian ethics. Patrick Henry, after all, said that the country was founded on the gospel of Jesus Christ, Kemple told me. "The founders understood that Christianity would be the accepted religion in America, and I really, fully believe that," he said, and added, "The citations, I got a bunch of them." Kemple then quoted from pro-Christian-nation propaganda that had been debunked repeatedly, even by conservative Christian scholars at universities.[23]

Kemple took center stage when the Steinbrenner issue moved from the blogosphere to the Hillsborough County School Board meeting room. Anywhere from a few to fifty people regularly signed up to speak against CAIR in January, February, March, and April, and Kemple was there every time, always using the same eye-catching tactic during the public comment period. He turned to the audience sitting behind him and announced, "I would like to ask everyone who is here because you don't want CAIR in the classroom to stand up briefly."[24] He would state matter-of-factly that CAIR had links to terrorism. His followers were more pointed in expressing their distrust and hate of the Muslim influence in America.

Miliziano, with her father sitting next to her for support, stayed long enough to hear hate directed at Muslims at one board meeting, then slipped out. She did not want to draw attention to herself or risk ending up in a photo. As the issue escalated, she began to have self-doubt, she confided to me in one of our early conversations. She wondered, "What am I doing? Have I ended my career? I've been teaching for twenty-seven years. Do I really need this?" She found strength in support from her school's leaders and from teachers throughout the school system. In an e-mail, a social studies teacher from Freedom High School thanked Miliziano for "taking a stand against the racial stereotypes that Muslims across America have been facing. I am a teacher at Freedom, a Muslim woman (who does wear a head scarf), and to hear that there are people in our education system doing what you did, makes me feel great (Muslim or not!). . . . Thanks again and stay strong!!!"[25]

The February 28, 2012, school board meeting was the most contentious. More than forty people signed up to speak about CAIR and about guest-speaker guidelines, now on the agenda as an information item. The themes of the opponents were the same. CAIR, they contended, was a threat against children, the country, and Americans' freedom. There were attacks on the organization, on Shibly, and on the school system for not protecting the children, and most of the CAIR opponents wore red shirts to show their solidarity.[26] "Why? Why would you allow CAIR, a known terrorist organization, to have the ability to have access to our children in our schools?" asked an early speaker, a member of Kemple's education coalition. A Baptist minister, the first pro-CAIR/pro-Shibly speaker to speak at a board meeting, recalled how the United States imprisoned Japanese families during World War II and how it took decades for the country to acknowledge it had overreacted. "I thought perhaps we had learned from our mistakes and would never fall into a trap of ostracizing a whole section of our society," he said. "Now I see groups trying to demonize a whole group of our society because they're Islamic." He made a plea for all faiths to work together. So did leaders of area civil rights organizations and a Muslim father of four.

Tension grew as a few speakers predicted they would oust school board members during the next election if the board didn't adopt strict guest-speaker guidelines and keep such organizations away from children. "This is not about race and it's not about religion," said a speaker, who at one point in his statement raised his voice and pounded a finger on the lectern. "It's about protecting our children from a group that advocates hate and violence to settle their differences. CAIR is known for this. We didn't put them on a terrorist watch list. The government did." People in the room whooped and applauded.

The animosity peaked when twenty-year-old Laila Abdelaziz, a senior at the University of South Florida, in Tampa, stepped up to speak. Her voice soft yet confident, she announced that she would read a unity prayer she had delivered at a prayer gathering in Washington, DC, after US Representative Gabrielle Giffords of Arizona was shot. Abdelaziz, when she first delivered the prayer, was interning for a US senator from Florida and represented the Muslim congressional staffers association. With large sunglasses perched on top of her head and long, black, flowing hair, she had an air of glamour and poise. But as she began to read the prayer, some members of the audience made side comments and others walked out. Abdelaziz kept reading what she had come to say, a statement reminding the audience that America was meant to be for everyone, "a nation that upholds and embraces religious rights and freedoms." When she walked back to her seat, she sensed the glare of those people in the red shirts and saw some shaking their heads as if to say, "Who is this girl and what does she think she just said?"

Still in her senior year in college in 2012, Abdelaziz had just started a job as the Tampa-based regional director of Emerge USA, a nonprofit, nonpartisan group working to give Muslim Americans a voice in the political process. Born in the town of Ramallah on the West Bank in the Palestinian territories, she went to high school in Ocala, about one hundred miles north of Tampa. She experienced derision and saw it happen to others, including a Muslim boy her history teacher nicknamed Aladdin.[27] As a college sophomore, she faced hecklers in 2010 as she posed a question to President Obama during a nationally televised town hall meeting in Tampa. She asked Obama to explain why America had not yet condemned Israel for its treatment of Palestinians and had to shout to make herself heard. The president motioned the audience to quiet, saying, "Wait a minute. Tampa, we can all get along here."[28] That was a tough moment, but there was something even more unsettling at the school board meeting. Those stares, those stares from the people in red, were creepy.

The thirty-seventh speaker of the night was Kemple, who made it clear that he and his followers would return if the school board did not act. He noted that Shibly was scheduled to speak next. "I'm sure that's not by accident, so he can counter it," Kemple said. "Address our concerns and look at the facts."

Then, Shibly walked up to the front of the room, stood at the lectern, and wasted no time expressing his frustration. "With everything that's been said, I'm just waiting for the marshal to jump out at any moment and arrest me," he said and held out his hands as if to mime getting handcuffed. "My name is Imam Hassan Shibly. From those who know me, from those who know CAIR, they have nothing but good things to say about us. Unfortunately, the reality is there has been so many lies said against us today that I feel like I have to come out and say the world isn't flat." Some of his supporters in the school system had hoped Shibly would speak gently, but he was too angry to be meek. He had heard others malign him and his organization for weeks. He had been accused of indoctrinating school children, of being a terrorist, and of running an organization that supported terrorism.

Still, he included a plea for understanding, for respect for Muslims simply trying to live productive lives in America. "We cannot let those who are promoting hatred and bigotry raise a flag of victory over our schools. Thank you, and God bless you. God bless America." Driving home to his wife and children that night, he felt tears come to his eyes for the first time since his visits to Steinbrenner had made news.[29]

After a few more speakers, the school board meeting shifted to the superintendent and board members, who seemed at cross-purposes. Superintendent MaryEllen Elia had given each board member a one-page sheet suggesting guest-speaker guidelines. In this first stab at such guidelines, the administration recommended that teachers make sure each guest speaker had the right experience and credentials to have a scholarly discussion of the topic at hand. Plus, representatives of advocacy groups would not be considered appropriate, since speakers should be there to educate, not advocate. The guidelines also called for teachers to give principals a speaker's name, credentials, and subject matter and to work with guests to create an outline of the presentation. At the time, the guidelines were much looser. All teachers had to do was pick a speaker and let the principal know someone was coming.[30]

Board members began debating the merits of the proposed guidelines. One member said he would support only a policy that dealt directly with how comparative world religions would be handled in the classrooms. He said he preferred that a teacher teach the material and thought it was not always or often necessary to bring in an outside speaker on religion. Candy Olson, the chairman, disagreed, saying she supported the idea of guest speakers on religion and worried that the controversy was having a chilling effect on teachers. Olson, a Catholic who belonged to Bridge Builders, a Tampa group of Christian, Muslim, and Jewish women, had blasted speakers in previous meetings for insulting teachers so blatantly, for making it seem as if the county's teachers were too stupid and too uninformed to know how to guide students and pick speakers. But by late February Olson had agreed to hold a board workshop just to discuss guest-speaker guidelines. A workshop was scheduled for late March with the caveat that there would be no public comment.

So at a regular board meeting three days before the workshop, the march of CAIR opponents continued. One of the twenty-one anti-CAIR, anti-Shibly speakers made remarks that many recall as the most odious during the controversy. She was open about her distaste for Islam. "It is not tolerance when we make deals with the devil. . . . There is no talk of Hindus and any other religions because the other religions don't teach hate, they don't teach that God is ashamed of women, that they need to be covered up like pigs in a blanket," she said, adding, "The Bible has warned us of this great day. You are being deceived. Islam is not a religion of peace. They are a religion of Jihad, and in the Koran, they teach it's okay to lie to the enemy, and guess what, any religion that is not Islam is the enemy. Coexist? Please."

At home, Miliziano watched the speakers via streaming video. All along, she had debated with herself whether the speakers' main concern was CAIR or Islam. Now, she knew the answer. It was about hate toward Muslims, hate in the form of a woman comparing Muslim women in hijabs to pigs in a blanket, and hate in the form of a man who accused Shibly of seducing innocent youngsters to become Muslims and who said Christianity was love while Islam promoted honor killings of young women. It was the very hate she and her colleagues tried to prevent through education.

At Steinbrenner, several of her colleagues were so incensed by the public hostility that they became even more determined to keep bringing in guest speakers on religion, including speakers from CAIR. Shelli Barton, who had taught for fourteen years in Tampa schools, was there when Shibly spoke to six of her world history classes. She believed Shibly brought something special because he was hip, young, and devout. He also added a layer to Islam that the teachers could not by talking about how he tried to live his life as an observant Muslim in such an advanced, materialistic world. Barton turned the controversy over Shibly's visit into a lesson about politics because her students kept bringing up the issue. A few students followed the blog posts and reported back to the entire class, then pushed Barton to discuss the publicity. She and her students talked about what was truth and what was fiction. They concluded that many bloggers were publishing propaganda, material the students and teacher labeled mental terrorism because the writers were trying to scare people into changing the way they felt.[31]

That people accused Shibly of indoctrination particularly infuriated students. One student who was in Miliziano's class was so upset that he wrote a letter to the *Tampa Tribune* about how Shibly's presentation on Islam was perfectly appropriate. "I don't feel like

I was being converted and certainly don't feel I was being 'brain-washed,'"[32] the student wrote. Neither did Laura Gonzalez. Shibly's talk helped cement for her the idea that Muslims were not bad people but that they just came from a religion, like any other religion. If anything, she wanted more instruction about religion and wished that her teachers also taught about lesser-known religions, like the Jehovah's Witnesses. While she now considered herself agnostic, her family members were Jehovah's Witnesses. Laura went to Kingdom Halls earlier in her childhood and still goes to the worship spaces on major holidays. Peers responded with scorn when they found out she was involved with the Jehovah's Witnesses and did not even understand that her religion was a branch of Christianity. They asked her questions like, "Oh, do you believe in God?" Her answer: "We're not a cult." Her own experiences made her all the more upset that others picked on Shibly.[33] Miliziano's class, though, was not a world religions class per se. It was world history, and if the teachers found time to talk about a smattering of major religions, they usually felt as if they had done their job. Even in a comparative religion class, teachers could not talk about every religion that existed. Maybe, though, teachers could find a way to address the issue Laura raised. Jehovah's Witnesses consider themselves a part of Christianity, but mainstream Christians don't often accept that. Mormons also have faced derision, as have many offshoots of various religions.

Seeking more students' views, I met with a handful in the school newspaper's closet-sized office. The paper's editor in chief, Samantha Bequer, who is Catholic, is part Cuban and part Native American. She made a halfhearted joke about the lack of respect for differences in race and religion within the school and outside of it. She quipped that she was the "resident brown girl" at her school, "one of the brave, the few." She could not believe some of the ill-informed comments she had heard, such as students saying, "Obama is so Muslim." Some students also acted as if their religions were superior and a few Baptists told her Catholics were not

Christian. A fellow staffer on the paper, who was Jewish, added that every year someone tried to convert him and told him he was going to go to hell because he was Jewish and did not believe in Jesus. I had to urge Samantha and other students in the newspaper office to take turns when they began talking about their frustration with the public outcry. Months later, they were still peeved about the response to Shibly's visit.

"I'm defending the fact that I'm not a dumb seventeen-year-old kid who's going to be brainwashed from one sitting," Samantha said. "I want to defend the fact that I'm an educated person and I have the right to listen to what I want to and that I'm not dumb. My teachers aren't dumb. My school is not dumb."

Sitting nearby, Rachel Evans spoke up. She had never met a Muslim before Shibly came to her world history class and believed he and the course was helping students shed their ignorance about religions. She was frustrated that strangers attacked Shibly when all he was doing was sharing his religion. To her, he gave the teens something beautiful.

The students' voice was largely silent publicly until March 30, 2012, when the board held its workshop about guest-speaker guidelines. The board invited a Steinbrenner sophomore to speak at the meeting and serve as an eyewitness to Shibly's talk. The boy was interviewed as if he were testifying in a trial.[34] He spoke matter-of-factly as he described how Shibly talked about the beginnings of Islam, Mohammed, the prophet's pilgrimage to Mecca, and the basic principles of the faith. At the end of the lecture, Shibly and the students had a question-and-answer session. Olson, the board chair, asked the student about the types of questions asked.

"We asked him about his beard and the hat he wore, and the laws about five times a day of prayer, and what would happen at school if Muslims needed to pray?" the boy recalled. "He said they could go to a special room."

"Do you feel there was any indoctrination?" Olson asked.

"No, ma'am," the student replied.

Stacy White, a board member who early on objected to the use of CAIR guest speakers, wondered if Shibly had talked about stereotypes and prejudice against Muslims.

"Oh, yeah, he just said there are a lot of stereotypes that all Muslims are terrorists and they don't like the United States, and this is in fact false. He said most of them don't feel that way," the student said.

Olson interjected: "He didn't say there were none?"

"Yes, obviously, you're going to have people who are radicals. It's the same with people of other religions. You're going to have those people willing to go to an extreme to prove their point," the student said, reminding me of the lesson Jonathan Rabinowitz taught the sixth graders in Wellesley about stereotypes as they began their four-week unit on Islam.

As the meeting drew to a close, Olson asked the board to reach a consensus on the value of speakers in the classroom before talking about guidelines. White wanted the board to talk more directly about the touchy issue of guest speakers on religion and to define what an inappropriate speaker or organization could look like. White objected, too, to the idea that a guest speaker would talk about stereotypes. "Why in the world were we talking about things like stereotypes in a class like world religions?" he asked. He questioned whether the district should set a policy requiring a guest speaker to be a professor or scholar whose academic credentials have been vetted. He did not believe that being an ordained cleric qualified someone to be a guest lecturer, a view shared by many religion scholars I had spoken with in recent years.

Olson handed out a new version of guidelines. Gone was the part that would have eliminated advocacy groups' representatives from visiting classrooms. By the meeting's end, the board directed the superintendent to revise the guidelines. A few days later, the controversy took one of its oddest turns. Caton, in reaction to what he viewed as the board's inaction at the workshop, offered a $3,000 reward to anyone providing tips about future speaking presentations by CAIR representatives at Steinbrenner. He e-mailed the news of his reward to Steinbrenner's staff and went one step further. He paid for a billboard near Steinbrenner to advertise the reward, promising $1,000 for the tip and another $2,000 if the notice came a week or more in advance.[35] Miliziano saw the billboard and she and Shibly couldn't resist joking about it. Perhaps she would invite him back and they could split the reward?[36]

A few weeks later, at the April 10 school board meeting, the superintendent showed up with revised guidelines. Now there was no mention of advocacy groups because barring them would prohibit too broad a list of organizations. The guidelines also included a recommendation from a teacher's guide on religion in the public schools, a 2008 national report a board member had referenced at the board workshop. The report recommended that if a school invites guest speakers on religion, it should look for someone with the right academic background to give an objective, relevant discussion of the historical period and religion. Use local college faculty as speakers or ask them for recommendations, the report advised. And it included a caution about religious leaders, saying schools should remember that clergy have allegiance to their own faith.[37] The guidelines passed.

As the 2011–2012 school year ended, Miliziano was hopeful she could invite Shibly back the next fall. She had had other Muslim speakers in the past, but the young Muslim man was better. He was lively, articulate, passionate, and knowledgeable because he had studied with Islamic scholars to become an imam. As the school year began, Caton again paid for a billboard offering rewards for tips about CAIR speakers at Steinbrenner. Then on September 11, 2012, the eleventh anniversary of the World Trade Center attacks, Kemple hosted a rally in front of the school system headquarters to renew the call for a policy to keep CAIR speakers out of the public schools. He stood with about thirty supporters, including the leader of the Boston-based Americans for Peace and Tolerance group that opposed the Wellesley field trip; the school board member who had objected to CAIR speakers; and members of other groups pledging to rid America of radical Islam. About as many people who supported CAIR tried to outshout Kemple's group.[38]

Given the atmosphere in fall 2012, Shibly told Miliziano that perhaps he should not return that year. So the teachers invited a different Muslim speaker, a teacher who also was on the board of CAIR. In fall 2013, speakers representing Buddhism, Hinduism, and Eastern Catholicism spoke to students. CAIR opponents seemed to have faded out of the picture, though Kemple soon would announce his third bid for a school board seat. As the school year continued, Miliziano still wanted to have a Muslim speaker when she started teaching students about Islam in 2014 and Shibly remained her top choice.[39]

When I came to Steinbrenner that February, Shibly had accepted Miliziano's invitation to speak, pending the principal's approval. The teacher, though, worried about whether she had made the right decision in inviting him. "I know how absolutely fierce and irrational Terry Kemple's crusade can become. I would knowingly flame the fires," she said to me during a break between classes. She predicted that her principal would say no.

The next day, after classes ended, Kelly King, now the principal at Steinbrenner, let me sit in as Miliziano talked about her desire to have Shibly return that week. Miliziano described how Shibly had just gotten back from a pilgrimage, making it a perfect time for students to hear about his experiences. "He said, 'Of course if you don't feel comfortable with me, we'll find somebody else,'" Miliziano told King. "I said, 'You know what? You'll come in. We won't publicize anything.'"

The principal said she was surprised that Shibly was so comfortable returning to the school. Miliziano noted that CAIR's role was to send in speakers. "Anyway, is it okay?" she asked.

"Absolutely," King said. Miliziano was stunned by the fast answer. So was I.

After getting her principal's approval, Miliziano walked into her colleague Barton's classroom and delivered the news that Shibly could come. Barton grinned and cheered but the teachers' celebration would be short-lived. Back in the principal's office, King was filled with doubt after Miliziano's exit.[40] She went to another meeting and began wondering if she would later regret the decision, particularly if Shibly's return ended up on the six o'clock news. She consulted the school's previous principal, who said that if she were in King's shoes she would bring in a different speaker. King knew Kemple was running for school board again. "He'd have a field day with it. Why go create that and give somebody a platform?" King told me as she defended her ultimate choice not to have Shibly back that year. The next morning, Miliziano and her colleagues looked glum during a break between classes. "We are disappointed that a small group could hijack our school. Kelly King was very clear about it: Not now," Miliziano said.

That evening, I met again with Shibly, who had offered to give me a tour of some of the area's mosques. He was surprised that Steinbrenner had withdrawn its invitation to him to speak. He thought of fighting the decision but decided not to because he did not want to make a problem for Miliziano. Disinviting him gave in to anti-Islam bigots, he said, and granted them more power.

We got into his four-door Acura ILX parked outside CAIR-Florida headquarters and made our first stop at the Islamic Society of Tampa Bay, one of the area's older mosques, with a health clinic in the back. Palm trees nearly hid the gold dome topping the minaret. This mosque, unlike those I had visited in the Boston area, had labeled women's and men's entrances. The women's prayer space was in a glass-enclosed area. As Shibly drove me to two more mosques, he talked about his own experiences seeing other houses of worship when he was young. He remembered visiting a large church and seeing girls in miniskirts. So unused to that in a worship space, he wondered how the boys could avoid being distracted during prayer. He wanted his own children to learn about other religions and saw nothing to fear from such exposure.

As he stood on the grounds of another mosque, known as Mas-jid al-Jami, he described how up to about five thousand Muslims regularly came there for prayers during Ramadan and how the over-flow of worshippers stood outside. "It is in society's best interest that people don't grow up scared of each other. I want a society where children of all faiths can grow up being proud of who they are and not feel threatened or harassed because of their religious identity," he said, speaking quickly, as usual, in his passion to make every point he could. Could going on a tour like this change detractors' harsh views of Shibly? But when offered an invitation to meet, his foes did not respond, he said. "You're getting the VIP Muslim tour," he added as he drove by the American Youth Academy, a private Islamic school near a mosque. He shouted a greeting in Arabic to a man walking out of the school then got out of the car to greet the man, who was the vice principal. Shibly pulled off his kufi so the school administrator could see his shaved head, a sign that he had recently done the hajj, the pilgrimage to Mecca that Muslims are obligated to do once in their lifetime. They believe the trip copies a trek the prophet Mohammed made with his followers. The vice principal smiled and rubbed Shibly's head as he congratulated him. Back in the car, Shibly gave an impromptu lecture about the hajj, talking about how pilgrims need to be pure. They are not supposed to wear perfume. They wear white. They stay focused on the spiritual, and to break out of that state, they have their heads shaved at the end at one of the makeshift barbershops put there for the occasion.

Next, we parked in front of a year-old mosque in a suburban area called New Tampa. Built in the Turkish style, the mosque had two minarets with copper domes. Inside, a two-way mirrored par-tition at the back of the sanctuary served as the entrance to the women's prayer space. But when it was time for the call to prayer, the imam and Shibly told me I could watch from a chair off to the side. Like in all mosques, there were no images of people but there were adornments, such as verses from the Koran inscribed over the mihrab in bold lettering surrounded by geometric designs in orange, red, and blue and a multi-tiered chandelier of gold and crystal shimmering at the bottom of a gold chain. Shibly had told me I did not need to cover my head but I was thankful that Miliziano had lent me a scarf. It felt right to cover my unruly, dark-blond-and-graying hair and respect the practices of this holy place. After the worshippers finished their prayers, Shibly introduced me to the imam. Then the pair talked about the imam's four-month-old baby and the discussion the imam and his wife had had about the baby's name. Opponents painted Shibly as the representative of terrorist groups, but members of his own community looked at him differently, as the face of the future of Muslims in America and as someone determined to build bridges between faiths. Shibly ended the tour at Petra, a Middle Eastern restaurant. Many women entered the restaurant in hijabs, and our waitress also wore a head scarf. Some women wore no head covering. The restaurant, like the mosques I had just seen, showed the diversity of the Muslim community in practices as well as the native countries of worshippers. We ate a lamb dish and hummus with pita and ended the meal with steaming cups of peppermint tea.

The next day was my last in Tampa, and at Miliziano's invitation I accompanied Steinbrenner world history students on their annual field trip to the Epcot theme park at Walt Disney World. The students' academic task was to work with partners to study one country's exhibit and look for evidence of social, political, cultural, and economic traits. Students were to consider religion when they looked for cultural traits. On the bus from Tampa to Orlando, I talked to two Muslim students, both sophomores in world history classes. I had to ask teachers' help finding Muslims at Steinbrenner because the school had only a handful. Miliziano told me about a student named Al Nafea because Al had objected to a guest speaker's depiction of Islam that fall. The guest speaker was an Eastern Catholic from Lebanon brought in to talk about a lesser-known branch of Catholicism. That the man came from Lebanon, Miliziano thought, broadened students' views of religions in the Middle East, but Al still smarted from what the man had said. The speaker made comments about Muslims' ill treatment of women, talking about how girls were forced to marry at age nine. Al saw those comments as promotion of negative stereotypes and had cringed at the man's depiction of Muslims. The fifteen-year-old said nothing during the class. But he had wanted to, the slender, soft-spoken teen told me as we sat in the narrow, high-backed bus seat. As the man spoke badly of Muslims, Al kept thinking to himself that he was being attacked and he could not do a thing.[41] He brooded about what the man said and told his friend, Hepah Hussein, about the comments. Hepah, also a sophomore and more outspoken than her friend, agreed to accompany Al as he went to express his concerns to Miliziano. He told the teacher that he did not believe the speaker represented Muslims fairly.

Miliziano, who agreed that the speaker overgeneralized, told Al the speaker had given his own perspective as a Christian from the Middle East. The day after Al complained, Miliziano spoke to her students about the speaker and reiterated that the man's view was his own perspective. She also talked to the speaker, who said he had not meant to offend anyone with his remarks. Al remained unsatisfied. Teachers, the teen said, should pick more-neutral speakers and be sure their content was fact-based rather than opinion-based. He also wasn't sure a speaker from CAIR was the right choice to talk about Islam. Maybe, he said, it would be better to stay away from someone attached to such a controversial group. Al wanted his peers and others to learn about Islam and know that his faith was peaceful. He did not deny that radicals existed and said he was no different from others fearful of terrorists. He did not like radicals, either, the teen told me in a voice barely audible above the roar of the bus's engine. He brought up an issue I struggled with after hearing about the Tampa controversy and also after seeing the guest speakers in Wellesley. Who could be a neutral speaker for a particular faith? Were parents, who were not necessarily experts on their own religions, good choices? Were religion scholars, who may or may not be as dynamic as laypeople or clergy, better picks?

Al was born in Tampa. He considered himself Palestinian American because his mother was born in the Palestinian territories and his father's parents came from there as well. He tried to keep his religion private. If someone asked, he would say he was Muslim. Otherwise, he just wanted what all teens desired, to blend in, and it was no easy task because he followed his religion's prohibition against dating, smoking, and drinking. He felt that Muslims at his school had almost no voice, and that his protest about the Lebanese Catholic speaker had proven that. There had been no public outcry about a guest speaker making anti-Muslim comments in a public high school. Miliziano planned to invite the same speaker back but said she would warn the man not to overgeneralize. Shibly was lambasted not for what he'd said but for what others believed he stood for.

Hepah, also fifteen, believed Shibly should be allowed to return to Steinbrenner. Her voice was laced with sarcasm as she marveled over people's claims that Shibly was trying to convert kids. "Like, wow, come on people, really? He wasn't even trying to bring a message like that to them. He was just trying to educate," Hepah said.[42] Like Al, she was born in Tampa and identified herself as Palestinian American. Her family originally came from the Palestinian territories but left because of the Israeli occupation of their homes, she said. Hepah beamed as soon as she met me, saying she was excited because no one had asked to hear her story before. She talked about going on errands with her mother, who wears a hijab, and getting looks from strangers, as if mother and daughter were outsiders. Hepah, though her father would like her to, had not committed to covering her long, black, curly hair. She told her father to let her finish high school first and then she would be stricter. She was unsure how her friends would treat her if she started wearing a hijab.

For her, issues began in the sixth grade, on the first day of middle school, when a boy in geography class poked fun at her last name.

"Oh, is your dad Saddam Hussein? Are you going to bomb a building?" the boy said. Hepah sat in silence for a moment, then said, "Shut up." She spoke with her father about it after school, and he advised her to first deal with it on her own and tell the boy to back off. If the boy persisted, he said, then involve the teacher. The boy teased her two more times in the same way, so Hepah told the teacher, who put a stop to it. Such incidents made her stronger and more determined to learn as much as she could about her religion so she could answer other students' questions correctly and confidently. She saw herself as setting an example for her peers of what a Muslim was. She prayed five times a day, fitting in prayer before and after school. Her father had left it up to her to decide when she was ready to date. Dating, though, had a different meaning to observant Muslims. It meant her father would bring men to the house for Hepah to check out and then either her father or her brother would accompany her and the suitor on their first date. She suspected she would not date until after college, and she wanted to study medicine. She told boys in high school she did not think it was right to date now. "They're like, 'Oh, okay,'" she said with a nervous giggle.

When we got off the bus at Epcot, Hepah and her two project partners let me tag along as they toured the France exhibit and made a video of a skit about the country. Hepah dressed the part of an American tourist for the skit and wore a Washington, DC, sweatshirt, jeans, and black sneakers. Around her neck, she wore a chain with a charm of a crescent moon and a mosque, a gift from her father after he did the hajj. "Are you familiar with the five pillars of Islam?" Hepah asked when I admired the necklace. I said yes, and she said her father had completed the hajj, the fifth pillar. I asked if she would make the same pilgrimage, and she said yes, with whomever she marries. Then, her attention diverted, she pointed at a minaret on a nearby building. "Is that Morocco?" she asked, adding that she was anxious to see the Moroccan exhibit because of the Islamic influence on the country. "Can we go to Morocco when we're done?" she asked her partners. One partner, Katie Wadler, nodded, but the other, a boy, declined. He preferred to go on rides.

With Hepah assuming the role of tour guide, the girls walked on to Morocco. Katie and Hepah, who had two classes together, met at the start of the school year and became friends. Katie, who is Jewish, could relate to her Muslim friend's story about what it was like to be in the religious minority at Steinbrenner. In eighth grade, some peers made a crack about Jews and money when she dropped a penny. Katie grew up in a family well aware of the worst of anti-Semitism. Her grandfather fled Germany as a child during the Holocaust. Katie became Hepah's enthusiastic student as the pair walked through Disney's Morocco. Hepah pointed at the geometric designs on a building and noted that they were common on mosques as well as on other buildings in the Middle East. They entered the exhibit's bazaar and Hepah became giddy with excitement at the sight of shops that resembled markets in the Palestinian territories. She and Katie stopped at a sign with Arabic phrases and Hepah taught the pronunciation for Arabic greetings. Inside a shop, Hepah held up a package of *bakhoor*, an incense her mother uses at home, and described how her mother puts it in a wooden, boat-shaped holder and burns it to fill the house with scent. Later, she showed Katie a package of *zatar*, a spice her aunt and grandmother make from scratch from their herb garden in Jordan. They dip bread in olive oil with the spice and eat it at breakfast. Back in another Moroccan shop, Hepah greeted the sales clerks in Arabic and asked them questions about Morocco because she had never been there. Then, another Epcot visitor walked up and asked the clerks in English, "Is Morocco the one that has the magic carpet?" After the woman walked away, the pair of teens rolled their eyes. Of all the questions one could ask about Morocco, asking about something connected to the movie *Aladdin* seemed lame. Then again, it was Disney World.

They debated whether to get henna tattoos before they left the Moroccan exhibit. Hepah flipped through plastic-covered pages of designs and ruled it out because the choices were too commercial. Mickey Mouse, in fact, was incorporated into several of the designs. She offered to take Katie to a henna place in Tampa. They walked through the park, stopping at souvenir shops and posing for selfies as they donned hats from China and Mexico. Muslim and Jew, they were aware of their religions' prickly relationship. Did their history class make it possible for them to create such a bond or was it their parents' openness? All Katie knew was she would not have felt comfortable asking Hepah about Islam if she didn't know her. Both girls wished their schools had begun teaching them about the world's religions much earlier.

Katie's mother, Joan Wadler, took it upon herself to provide some of that earlier education after noticing an exclusive emphasis on Christmas in her children's elementary schools. When her daughter was in kindergarten, the children made Christmas trees out of construction paper. She provided materials for her daughter to make a dreidel instead. Then, in the hopes of educating the students, Wadler began offering each year to talk about Hanukkah in her children's elementary classrooms. She brought in a menorah and a dreidel and read students a book about Hanukkah. No teacher ever turned down the mother's offer.[43]

CHAPTER FOUR

How Young Is Too Young?

ABOUT 1,350 MILES to the northwest, it was the teacher who led the lesson on Hanukkah. The six- and seven-year-olds sitting on the rug couldn't scoot close enough. They all wanted a good look at the silver candelabra their teacher cupped in her hands. Slender navy candles sat in nine holders that extended like branches of a tree. Tiny silver balls adorned its pedestal. "Ooh," several children squealed.

"A menorah," their first-grade teacher, Deborah Fagg, said as she stood holding it above the children's heads. Jews, she explained, did not light all the candles at once during Hanukkah. They added a candle each night and by the last night, every candle flickered with light.

"So what's it called?" she asked.

"A menorah," her twenty-two students recited. Many of them had never heard of or seen a menorah before.

It was mid-November 2013, but Fagg wasn't teaching about Hanukkah because the holiday was just a few weeks away. Giving the children a look at a menorah was a sliver of a half-hour lesson the teacher delivered that morning on Judaism. She was following the guidelines for the curriculum all first-grade teachers use at the Minneha Core Knowledge Elementary School in Wichita, Kansas.

Over a few weeks every fall, in mostly half-hour chunks, the first graders learn about the three major world religions in order of their founding, Judaism, Christianity, and Islam. They get the basics, the story of each religion's founding, the name of its house of worship, and symbols, holidays, and important figures.

A newspaper story about a Kansas school under fire for a display about Islam led me to Minneha. But this was not just a story about another war between educators and those who wanted schools to either ignore Islam or focus primarily on what they viewed as the religion's evils. This was a deeper story looking at just how early public schools could teach children about the world's religions and at the internal conflict devout Christian teachers faced when asked to give these lessons.

In this 640-student school in the middle of the Bible Belt, it was not left up to chance that a Jewish parent might offer to bring in a menorah and talk about Hanukkah or that a Muslim parent might volunteer to talk about Ramadan. At Minneha, since 1998, it had become the teachers' responsibility to teach about different religions' holidays and not just focus on the Christian ones, an obligation some embraced and others met with discomfort. The first-grade teachers at the school were all Christian and so were most of their colleagues in other grades. As elementary teachers, they were not necessarily schooled in the world's religions.

In numerous interviews, teens from around the country told me they wished their schools had started teaching them about religion much earlier. The bullying and misunderstandings over religion started about the time children entered school. The teens saw bringing the instruction in earlier as a possible solution. But was it a solution good for all schools regardless of locale? The superintendent of Lumberton, Texas, schools told me he doubted such an idea would fly in his town. Wichita was not as isolated or homogenous as tiny Lumberton, but it was still in a conservative part of the nation. As I drove down a highway in Wichita, an electronic billboard flashed a gigantic message: "Come this Sunday, Evolution, the Great Lie, Part

4, with Pastor Terry Fox." Fox, a Southern Baptist pastor, oversaw a congregation of around six thousand at the Summit Church. He had led the effort to pass a state constitutional amendment banning same-sex marriage in Kansas and had been equally fervent about trying to get the state to offer opposing theories to evolution in the classroom.[1]

Some longtime Wichitans say the city of roughly 386,000, the largest in the state, grew even more conservative after the "Summer of Mercy" in 1991, when Operation Rescue moved its headquarters to the city and ran six weeks of protests against the city's three abortion clinics, claiming they were saving babies. The protesters' main target was an abortion clinic run by George Tiller, one of just four doctors in the nation who would perform late-term abortions for women whose health was in danger because of pregnancy. Thousands protested outside his clinic in 1991. Two years later, the doctor was shot in both arms. In 2009, an abortion opponent shot and killed Tiller as Tiller, serving as an usher, handed out church bulletins during Sunday services. By then, Tiller's clinic was the only abortion clinic remaining in Wichita.[2] I heard plenty of Tiller references during my time in Wichita. A Thai restaurant I ate at was just a few blocks from the church where Tiller was murdered. Minneha Elementary School was a few miles away. The Summer of Mercy and Tiller's murder were dark times in Wichita that had left a permanent stain.

Wichita outwardly can seem plain vanilla and commercial. I drove by parched-looking plains, saw an occasional horse stable and numerous billboards with signs for Denny's and a Bible supply store, and then passed a strip mall with a McDonald's, a Lowe's, an IHOP, and a Taco Bell. But the city had more diversity than met the eye. One of its iconic images was the *Keeper of the Plains* statue of a Native American in headdress at the fork of the Big and Little Arkansas rivers. The city, which had an African American history museum, touted itself as the site of the country's first civil rights sit-in. In July 1958, a group of young black high school and college students sat at the Dockum Drug Store every day for hours for more than three weeks before the owner finally agreed to serve them at the counter.[3] In the city's schools in 2013, only a third of the students were white, while the rest came from various racial and ethnic groups. Religious diversity showed in the array of houses of worship. A growing population of Hindus had recently built a temple in a nearby suburb. There were three mosques, a Jewish temple, and a Buddhist temple, along with churches of various denominations and sizes.

Wichita's first mosque opened on the west side in 1979 and had had rocky times in recent years. In October 2011, the mosque was set on fire and heavily damaged. Area churches offered their spaces for worship and other help, but the fire was a reminder of anti-Muslim sentiment that simmered among some in the community. Not long before the fire, the mosque had received letters calling the prophet Mohammed a pig and drawings mocking the founder of Islam. Muslims will not hang an image of Mohammed anywhere and it is considered particularly offensive to attempt drawings of the prophet.[4] In the fire's aftermath, many Wichita residents sent letters to the editor expressing sorrow and saying the mosque fire did not represent the community as a whole. They wanted Muslims to know they were welcome in Wichita. Area Muslims remembered the fire but told me they did not see it as a reflection of the entire community. The principal of an Islamic school housed in one of the city's eastside mosques described a cooperative relationship between the mosque and the church across the road. The two congregations share parking space and members visit each other's houses of worship to learn about each other. The principal expressed no anger toward the people who set the mosque on fire. He said those who degrade Islam were ignorant. "I really appreciate what you're doing because we need to get all of the religions together at the table. We are one small world," he said to me, then added, just before stepping into the mosque for evening prayer, "Take all of the pictures you want."[5] I tried to capture a particular image, of how the mosque with the black dome faced Wichita's Highway 96 on one side and a church on the other. But it was too hard to get it all in one frame, an image that showed two religions almost side by side.

Minneha in 2013 was the only public school in Wichita that taught students about the world religions at such a young age, though years ago a few other Wichita schools had offered the same program, known as Core Knowledge. One school closed because of funding issues; the other just stopped using the approach. Author and education researcher E. D. Hirsch Jr. created Core Knowledge, designed for prekindergarten to eighth grade. He began it with one school in 1991 and it has since spread to about 1,200, including 300 preschools, across the country. About 40 percent of the schools using Core Knowledge are public while the rest are private, including religious schools.[6] Hirsch, whose ideas have never been beloved by all in education circles, has long advocated that all children need to learn certain content in history, geography, literature, and other topics at various stages. The program Minneha uses spins off of a list of things that Hirsch says every student at a particular grade level should know, and he includes knowing about the world's religions as an integral part of studying history and geography. In first grade, students begin learning history with a quick look at the Ice Age and move on to learning about two of the earliest civilizations in Africa.[7] They start in ancient Egypt and learn about that long river called the Nile, as well as pharaohs. They get an early taste of religion and an idea of how the ancient Egyptians believed in many gods. Next, they learn about Mesopotamia and hear the story of Gilgamesh and about how the Mesopotamians, like the ancient Egyptians, worshipped numerous gods. That sets the stage for them to learn about Judaism, Christianity, and Islam, the first major religions with a belief in one God. In second grade, as part of learning about early Asian civilizations, they study Hinduism and Buddhism. In third grade, they focus on the development of ancient Rome, which would include more about Christianity. In fourth grade, they focus on the Middle Ages and the

Holy Wars, returning to learn more about the spread of Islam. In fifth grade, they learn about the Mayans and other ancient civilizations.[8]

While Wichita uses Core Knowledge in just one school, Oklahoma City went from using it in twenty-nine of its elementary schools to trying to phase in the approach in all fifty-five. But how well these schools implement the curriculum varies, as does whether they include the portion about religions. Some principals have questioned the point of including instruction about religion when state tests don't ask questions about it.[9] Hirsch's curriculum got a big boost in recent years when New York State agreed to adopt it for reading instruction in elementary schools and piloted the reading materials, also used at Minneha, in ten New York City schools. Some education researchers remain skeptical, though they don't home in on the religious part. Diane Ravitch, a former US assistant secretary of education, has said Hirsch expects far too much of first graders by requiring them to understand facts, concepts, and places usually not taught until middle and high school.[10]

Minneha was a school in turmoil when it adopted Core Knowledge in the late 1990s. It then had 750 students crammed into two building, test scores were abysmal, and the atmosphere was chaotic. Administrators decided to transform it into a magnet school with a clear focus, and a conservative school board member promoted Core Knowledge, seeing it as a way to bring religion back into the schools.[11] The board member thought Hirsch, often depicted wrongly as an educator who favored teaching only European history, had created a curriculum perfect for conservatives. Some board members heard the reference to religion and did not realize that teachers would be asked to teach about several religions, not just Christianity. The board approved the change for Minneha, which also underwent renovations. Its student body, following the philosophy of magnet schools, became more diverse. Today, the school, located almost in the shadow of the Hawker Beechcraft airplane-manufacturing company on a four-lane road, enrolls 40 percent of its children from the neighboring areas and 60 percent from around the city. Its student population is almost evenly split among Hispanics, Asians, blacks, and whites.

The first principal to oversee Core Knowledge toed the line on the goal regarding religion, which was to give equal time to the five religions studied over the years.[12] She worked hard to eliminate holiday celebrations during her years at Minneha and to remove overtly religious Christian songs from the Christmas concerts. The principal who had championed the new approach retired around 2003 and the school went through four principals in four years until 2007, when Linda Hope came and stayed. Test scores had fallen again by the time Hope became principal and the veteran educator saw Core Knowledge as part of the solution, though she knew little about the program. The curriculum had now gained a reputation for improving children's test scores, based on studies in Oklahoma City.[13] But to make it work, schools had to embrace the whole philosophy. If a teacher skipped instruction on a topic in one grade, it would affect students' ability to learn more about the concept in the next grade. Some Minneha teachers embraced Core Knowledge from day one while others adopted it piecemeal. Hope worked to get teachers to use Core Knowledge fully so that it made sense to refer to Minneha as a Core Knowledge school. She liked the message that teaching about different religions carried, the idea that people needed to respect others' beliefs and practices. Like many of the school's teachers, she had grown up sheltered from other faiths. The only people she knew growing up in Kansas City were Catholics or Protestants and she didn't meet a Jew until she started college. The sixty-two-year-old principal knew even less about Muslims and learned on the job. Minneha has several Muslim families, and a parent a few years before had asked if the cafeteria could offer an alternative when pork was served because observant Muslims would not eat pork. Neither would Jews who kept kosher. The principal asked the cafeteria to offer peanut butter sandwiches, and now it offers several other options on days when pork is served.

Minneha, when Hope got there, was again using religious songs in Christmas concerts. She said no to "Silent Night" and urged teachers instead to find a mix of songs that represented religions taught across the Core Knowledge curriculum. When I visited with teachers at Minneha in late fall 2013, I sensed tension between teachers' deep fondness for their faith and the goal to treat several religions equally. A few teachers every year put Christmas trees in their classrooms and attached Santa decorations to their doors. A school administrator dressed up as Santa in recent years and middle school band members donned red elves' hats to perform Christmas concerts at the school. Most teachers grew up in Wichita or in small towns nearby. Deborah Fagg, the teacher who brought in the menorah, had come to the school eight years before to take her first job as a teacher after working for several years as a teacher's aide in her hometown of El Dorado. When she first came to Minneha, the school's downplaying of Christmas and Easter bothered Fagg. Her parents brought her up Baptist and she converted to Catholicism because her husband was Catholic. In the El Dorado elementary school where she used to work, she and the teachers made Easter egg baskets with the children and put Christmas trees in their classrooms and decorated them with the students. She missed those traditions when she first came to Minneha.[14] Fagg, though, soon grew to like the Core Knowledge approach and to respect the idea that it was better to teach about the diversity of religions than to promote just one.

Some of her colleagues still struggled to adapt and talked to me about how hard it was to tone down Christmas, in particular, in their classrooms. One, who came to teach at Minneha about twenty years ago, resented what she thought was happening not just at Minneha but at schools all over Wichita. Teachers could no longer talk about Jesus's birthday at Christmastime or sing the songs they used to. The country, she said, was trying so hard to honor other cultures in the world that it had forgotten about the customs in America. In her view, celebrating Christmas in school was one of them. "Amen," echoed a teacher sitting across from her.[15] Once again, like in Lumberton, I kept my opinion to myself. Some of the teachers did not seem to care how promoting Christmas might affect children who did not celebrate the holiday. And yet the teachers said they knew the boundaries in the classroom. The same teacher who pined for Christmas celebrations in school noted that the teachers never preached religion. They taught about different religions to help the children understand the world they live in. They talked about the nature of God and what that meant to civilizations over time. They did not promote one religion over another. They had varying views on whether to talk about their own religion with students. One did not reveal that she was Christian for fear her students would think she was pushing her religion. But Fagg and another colleague were open about it.

"I'm a Christian," Fagg said to me.

Fagg saw revealing her religion as part of building her relationship with her students. From the first day of school, she wanted her students to think of her and the rest of the class as one big family. Her Catholicism was just another in a string of facts they could learn about her. She was fifty-seven. She was the mother of three grown daughters. She was still married to her high school sweetheart, whom she wed at age eighteen. She went to community college after high school but didn't know what she wanted to do. She went back to college later in life and that's why she didn't start her teaching career until age fifty. Faith came first in her life and family second. Every morning, she prayed the rosary and listened to the prayer on the radio as she drove to work. She could not pretend to be something she was not but she thought she knew where to draw the line. It was not as if she talked about her faith every day in class.

A teacher's perception, however, may not always match parents' views. Fagg taught students how to write letters and numbers with rhymes she used when she was a special education teacher's aide. "Slide over in the sky, slant down from heaven," she said when she taught children how to make the number seven. A few years ago, a boy in her first-grade class at Minneha heard that and was confused. "What's heaven?" he asked. A classmate at some point said, "What, are you dumb? You don't know what heaven is."[16] Hearing this story from his son, the boy's father, Kyle Ecklund, was irate. "This being Kansas, eighteen kids knew all about heaven," the twenty-nine-year-old father said. Ecklund, an agnostic, and his wife, a Buddhist, had never talked to their son about heaven and had not made a decision about how they might, if at all, raise their children with a religion. Ecklund complained to the principal about Fagg's use of the handwriting rhyme. He considered it a promotion of a Christian concept. The principal agreed, saying she would frown on the use of religious rhymes to learn letters and numbers. Fagg told me she never knew a parent had complained, nor had she ever thought those rhymes would be a problem.

The father soon felt the school had dealt his family a double whammy. First, there were rhymes referencing heaven. Then, his son brought home worksheets about Christianity. He and his wife had applied to get their son into Minneha because they liked what they had heard about Core Knowledge at a districtwide fair about magnet schools. They did not remember hearing about the world religions part of the curriculum and their son now was asking questions about religion that they were unprepared to answer. Ecklund at first was furious because he just couldn't fathom that teachers were talking about religion in school. He thought educators had to keep a strict separation between church and state in every aspect of education. He did not know it was legal to teach about religion in the public schools.[17] After meeting with a school district parent liaison, his anger subsided. He examined the content and realized the curriculum's intentions, to teach children about the diversity of religions in the world, were good. But the father still did not like that he had been surprised. He suggested to Hope that the school do more to inform parents about the part of the curriculum involving religions, perhaps send parents a note a week before the unit began so parents could have discussions with their children ahead of time.

Maybe give parents a choice to opt their children out of the lessons if they wanted to. Treat it like schools do sexual education, basically. Ecklund was not sure he would keep his son out of the lessons but he wanted the choice.

Minneha had no uniform policy regarding telling parents about the religions unit. Some teachers sent letters home a week before the unit began and sometimes got responses like, "What do you mean you're going to teach about religion?" One parent didn't want her first grader to listen to anything about Judaism so her teacher let the student sit in the hallway during those discussions. Yet the same parent didn't object to lessons about other religions, including Islam. But opting out was not ideal because the curriculum was designed to be progressive. The Core Knowledge Foundation, which oversees the curriculum, in 2012–13 began providing sample letters for teachers to send home to parents of first graders. The letters explained how the teachers, who had just taught the children about Mesopotamia and ancient civilizations that believed in many gods, would next teach a series of lessons about Judaism, Christianity, and Islam. The letter emphasized that no religion would be singled out in any way that suggested that it was superior or more correct than another. Teachers' readings to students about each religion would be "presented in a balanced and respectful manner," the letter continued. If students, the letter noted, raised questions about the truth or rightness of any particular belief or religion, teachers would encourage the children to discuss that with their parents, saying, "People of different faiths believe different things to be true. These are questions you may want to talk about with your family and the adults at home."[18] The foundation created the letter out of an increasing sensitivity to different parts of the country using the curriculum. They did not want anyone to come back and say, "Whoops," the foundation's president told me.[19]

Even if Minneha sent parents a letter as a heads-up, Ecklund was not convinced that would resolve all of his concerns. He remained unconvinced that first grade was the right time to start the instruction.

His son reported back that he felt like an outsider because he knew so much less about Christianity than his classmates. The father tried to explain to his son that the world was home to hundreds of different religions and ideas and each had its own beliefs. His son, however, now thought Jesus was God. Ecklund did not blame Fagg. He thought the bigger problem could be what the rest of the class was saying. He could not help but wonder whether the teachers were skilled enough to manage the comments that could surface when religion took center stage in the classroom. He was not the only parent in the school with such worries.

Liz and Larry Karp were shocked when their son, Benjamin, came home from his first-grade class with worksheets and a quiz about the three main world religions. Benjamin's mother simply didn't think a first grader should be quizzed on what the Koran was or on the names of various religions' prophets. She considered it inappropriate for grade school, and she and her husband were particularly worried that lessons about religion would confuse their son because they were Messianic Jews. The Karps, who met while both were in the Air Force, chose the religion as a couple. She had grown up attending a Church of Christ congregation and already knew Jesus as lord. Larry Karp grew up in an interfaith family; his father was Jewish and his mother was Christian. Messianic Jews typically are Christians who believe Jesus is the messiah but also embrace many tenets of Judaism. Liz Karp described herself as a Christian who is Torah observant. Her husband, who wore a tallit under his clothes and a yarmulke, told me he retained a connection to his Jewish roots.[20]

The Karps have made a religious life for their son at home and at their congregation, L'chaim B'Yeshua, which means "To life in Jesus." On Saturdays, Benjamin studies at home with his father using a Bible written in Hebrew and English that has both the Old and New Testaments. I visited with the family in their living room, which could have been my own given all of the Judaica. On the wall was a painting of the Western Wall in Jerusalem, and a shofar and candleholders for Shabbat rested on the mantel. The Karps felt their son's elementary school was taking the responsibility for teaching about religion out of parents' hands. Upset about the first-grade worksheets, they spoke to Benjamin's teacher, and he was excused from the doing the work on religions in class. I asked Benjamin what he did instead. He told me he put his head down on his desk or did crossword puzzles. His voice had the soprano sound of a young boy, but his words were those of an older soul. He was, in fact, a year younger than most of his peers because he had started kindergarten at age four.

In second grade, Benjamin brought home coloring pages about Hindu gods, and his parents intervened again. In religious school, Benjamin had been learning that there was only one God and that he was not supposed to even speak of other gods. It gave the young boy the jitters to hear his teacher talk about Hindus' belief in multiple gods with different powers. His parents complained and Benjamin's second-grade teacher gave him alternative assignments. They asked for accommodations again during the annual winter concert. As Messianic Jews, the Karps did not believe in celebrating Christmas because they viewed it as a pagan holiday. So when the second grade sang Christmas songs, Benjamin stepped behind the stage curtain. He rejoined the chorus when they sang a few songs about Hanukkah. He liked that part, and he was even happier when his teacher let him talk about Hanukkah in the classroom and explain the meaning of the four letters on a dreidel. But he felt uneasy when required to learn about other religions. By the time he finished second grade, he and his parents had grown increasingly frustrated at the focus on learning about world religions at Minneha. For the Karps, the worst was to come.

On August 14, 2013, his first day as a third grader, Benjamin walked into Minneha and saw a huge bulletin board with an orange background on his way to his class. The seven-year-old's eyes widened at the sight of white pillars with the heading "Five Pillars of Islam." The fourth-grade teachers had put out bulletin-board displays to prepare for upcoming units and this bulletin board was blank except for its title and design. In upcoming weeks, the plan was for the fourth graders to fill the bulletin board with projects on Islam. Benjamin couldn't believe a big display on Islam was there on the first day of school.[21] He came home and told his mother it upset him. But he could not explain quite why.

The next day, Liz Karp went to Minneha, took a photo of the bulletin board, and told the assistant principal that the display made her son uncomfortable. She demanded to know why this display was in the main hallway. "Is this becoming like an Islamic school?" she asked. The administrator told her the display was for the fourth grade, scheduled to soon learn about the spread of Islam as part of history. That did not ease the mother's concerns. She could not understand why the school had to put up such a loud display and wanted to know what was taught about Islam. She wanted to make sure that the school was also teaching children about what she considered the dark side of Islam and the Muslims' hatred of Jews, in particular. Would the school, for example, teach the children that if they didn't bow to Allah they would be considered infidels, Liz Karp asked the administrator? She wanted to know, too, whether the school would teach the children that the Koran says to kill all infidels, and that one of Islam's precepts called for annihilating the Jewish faith. The assistant principal told the mother that no, the children would not be taught that.[22]

Dissatisfied, Liz Karp told the school she would take the matter to the superintendent. It wasn't just their son's discomfort that grated on the Karps. They believed the school was omitting critical information about Islam, namely, the sixth pillar, which the family said refers to jihad, the annihilation of the infidels. Every class I had observed, whether in elementary, middle, or high school, referred to five pillars, the widely held belief within Islam. The Karps were fervent in their belief that a sixth pillar had to be included. When the family didn't hear back from Wichita's superintendent, Liz Karp e-mailed a copy of the photo to a friend, also a state representative. He e-mailed the photo to a handful of other lawmakers, and the photo of the bulletin board display spread across the Internet. Once again, a school came under siege.

A group called Prepare to Take America Back posted the photo on its Facebook page with a heading "Students at Minneha Core Knowledge Elementary school in Wichata [*sic*] were met with this their first day. This is a school that banned all forms of Christian prayer. This cannot stand." More than 162,000 people liked the post on Facebook. *Bare Naked Islam*, which uses the subtitle "It isn't Islamophobia when they really ARE trying to kill you," became one of many blogs and websites that reran the photo and lambasted the school.[23] Hate e-mails, often laced with profanity, began flowing into the school and into school district headquarters. "Where the hell do you get off banning Christianity for Islam, you anti-America pieces of shit?" one person wrote in an e-mail sent from an iPhone to the school district. "You might as well hand them AK47s and strap a bomb to them. . . . May you all burn in hell." Yet another e-mailer wanted to know how Minneha could "promote that satanic cult of Islam in your school."[24]

Hope, the principal, had worked in education for forty years and had never experienced anything so venomous. That the Karps had started it surprised and frustrated her. She felt the school had accommodated the family's concerns from the moment they first complained. The principal was the main recipient of hate mail and threats. One day, she received an envelope addressed with beautiful handwriting and opened it to find photos of people hurting each other and a letter with nasty words directed at her. She also received boxes from anonymous sources. The school system put extra security outside the school for weeks, and Hope handed over the boxes, which the security guards opened and took away. One box had videotapes showing vile acts supposedly committed by Muslims.

Amid the hate, though, were glimmers of hope. A pastor of a local church sent a letter praising the school for its instruction about religions and dozens of his congregants signed it in support of Minneha. A woman sent an apology to the superintendent for at first jumping to the same conclusions as various websites. She thanked the school system for being responsible and allowing children to be educated about history and different cultures. Ecklund, the parent who had complained about his son learning about religion in the first grade, also stood up for Minneha when he gave an interview to a local television station. He saw no problem with the billboard and viewed the public outrage as anti-Islamic.

A few days after the photo went public, Minneha's principal sent a letter to parents. Hope mentioned how the school had visual representations of other religions besides Islam, including a painting of the Last Supper. She explained how religion was an important component of the history of civilizations and how Minneha students learned about five major religions of the world as part of a focus on history and geography. She emphasized the program's "teach, not preach" philosophy and noted how people had taken offense to the bulletin board without understanding the Core Knowledge curriculum. To alleviate the distraction to students and teachers, the display was taken down and would not reappear until the children began their study of Islam in October, she wrote.

Minneha, first attacked for having the display, now faced criticism for removing it. A column by Charles C. Haynes, the senior scholar at the First Amendment Center in Washington, DC, was picked up by newspapers around the nation. Haynes, long an advocate for schools teaching about religions, rapped the school, saying it had surrendered to ignorance and fear when it removed the display. "The suddenly empty space on the bulletin board sends a chilling message to students, parents, and teachers at Minneha and other public schools: Study about religions in a public school—no matter how fair and objective—can get you into trouble," Haynes wrote.[25]

—ᴡ—

On my trip to Wichita, I met with the fourth-grade teachers and they insisted they had not caved in to fear and ignorance. The teacher who had designed the display felt responsible, and her colleagues deferred to her. She felt the reaction to the display was too stressful and awful to risk going through again. So the teachers removed the white pillars and the heading that read "Five Pillars of Islam." They did not, though they had been expected to, restore the same display in October. Instead, in its place, still on an orange background, was a heading that read "Islamic Art," and teachers filled the space with students' paper replicas of plates, urns, and vases colored with geometric Islamic designs.

On a tour she gave me of the school, Hope pointed out the redone bulletin board and a new one nearby. This board was covered with paper and headlined "Spread of Islam." This bulletin board would not come down no matter what, the principal vowed. In a moment of whimsy, Hope took me to one of her favorite spots in the school, a wall where there was a poster of the University of Kansas mascot, a Jayhawk, encouraging children to drink milk. She posed for a photograph. It was one display that she knew would not cause consternation. Hope had not ordered the teachers to remove the display on Islam but understood their reasoning. The teachers were not just distracted by the uproar. They were afraid that someone might do something to the school if the display stayed up, and they had good reason to worry. One commenter on the Prepare to Take America Back site had suggested getting someone to smear bacon grease all over the bulletin board as a slam against Muslims, who do not eat pork if they are observant.

The bulletin board brouhaha played to the fears Minneha's fourth-grade teachers had had for years because they were the ones responsible for teaching the two-week unit on Islam. More than any other subject, Islam was the one unit they entered into with trepidation each fall. They knew about the unease over Islam in

America in the aftermath of 9/11. They knew, too, that some of the school's families had issues with instruction about religion in the earlier grades. Teaching about Islam also did not come naturally to the teachers. Wendi Turner, who had taught at Minneha for fourteen years, knew only what she had read in the news when she began teaching the unit. In the beginning, she was uncomfortable teaching about Islam. Turner, a Methodist who had grown up in Andover, a town east of Wichita, had to educate herself to become more knowledgeable about Islam. When the 9/11 attacks occurred, she was already teaching the religion unit, and it helped that she had Muslim students in her classroom. She looked at them and realized they were no different from her.

"They just pray to a different God," she said as we talked in a conference room after her classes ended. "They pray to Allah. I pray to God."[26]

Turner had just expressed the very notion that mainstream Muslims would like to dispel, that Allah was not the same as God in other religions.

"Do you see Allah as a different God?" I asked.

"To me, with my Christian beliefs, I see it differently. There is no face that goes with Allah. In my church, you see a face, of Jesus Christ," she said.

I did not debate her, but as a Jew who referred to God as "Adonai," a Hebrew word, in prayer, I could see little difference between that and Muslims saying "Allah." I wondered if Turner's beliefs made it hard for her to teach about Islam because the curriculum stressed that Allah was the Arabic name for God. She shook her head, saying it was not a problem because she could put her own religious beliefs aside. Besides, the more she learned, the more she realized that the three main world religions had many similarities, too.

When she taught about Islam, she was teaching history, not theology. The fourth graders learned about how, why, and where Islam spread, and the Muslim students in her class often became more open and willing to talk about their religion during the unit. They talked about how they practiced their faith and responded to their classmates' questions. In turn, the teacher became more educated as well. She realized that the pork taboo meant her Muslims students could not eat the marshmallows the class shot out of catapults from replicas of Middle Age castles. Gelatin, often one of the ingredients, can stem from pigs' bones. Turner had wanted her colleagues to keep up the same display about the pillars of Islam but compromised because of concerns about safety. She felt, though, that the bulletin board was a fair representation of the content of the unit. "Ignorance is stupidity. I'm not converting children," she said.

The principal, who fielded the calls, read the e-mails, and tried to shield the teachers, gained comfort from a cartoon in the *Wichita Eagle* by Richard Crowson. It depicted a bulletin board with the words "The bulletin board about the religion Islam has been blocked by a Facebook Page." In the cartoon, a handful of children stood nearby trying to analyze what had happened. "It was caused by a group that says they're 'taking America back . . ,'" one boy said, and a girl in glasses responded, "To what century?" The cartoon was a humorous respite for Hope. In Wichita, if you were in a Crowson political cartoon, you had really made it. When the e-mails began coming in, she told herself that she would not let this incident derail her education career. In the past, Hope had felt she could handle most problems on her own. She considered herself tough, a survivor not just of work battles but of life. She had gone through treatment for breast cancer some years ago. But the tone of the e-mails, the boxes, the barrage on the Internet against her and the school kept building. She called central office administrators for help. They responded to media inquiries, provided extra security, and advised her.

At the bottom of the cartoon that so amused Hope, a little dog had a thought balloon with the words "Wish cooler heads prevailed instead of hot Hedkes." Hedke was a reference to Dennis Hedke, the Kansas state representative who had passed along Liz Karp's photo to other lawmakers. He knew the Karps because they belonged to the same Messianic Jewish congregation of roughly sixty members. He commented early on about the bulletin board and told the Kansas Watchdog, a news site run by an independent journalist, that the news of the display appalled him when he first heard of it.[27] A few months later, he told me he was still just as appalled as we met in his office where he worked as a geophysicist and helped companies find locations to drill for oil.

Stacked against the rest of the angry activists I would meet over the years in Wellesley, Tampa, and Lumberton, Hedke was one of the smoothest talkers. It was easy to envision him mesmerizing the faithful at a state or even national political convention. With his Kansas twang, he had a folksy charm. He immediately tried to put me on the spot by asking me how I felt about Islam. I ducked the question, unsure of whether he would end the meeting if he realized I did not view Islam as a religion to revile. He reiterated what he said to the Kansas Watchdog but added a word he said had been left out: "just." "If you're going to talk about Islam and make it sound like it's just another one of those religions that needs to be understood and contemplated by mankind, there's a serious misunderstanding," he said. He echoed the Karps' stance, that the display left out the sixth pillar, of jihad, so that Minneha was teaching a skewed view of Islam at the fourth-grade level. He thought teaching about religion in the first grade was an even worse idea.

He spoke calmly, politely, his voice devoid of the anger that others had expressed in e-mails that flooded Minneha and the school system. He cited a common refrain of opponents to courses about religion, wondering why people could not say a prayer in public schools for fear of hurting someone's feelings but teaching about Islam was okay. I noted that Minneha taught about several religions, including Christianity, but he maintained he did not agree with the approach. "Linda, I have to ask you this question. What other religion on the face of this earth demands that their good patrons kill the infidels? There's a big difference between the rest of the world religions and that one," he said.

Viewing that question as rhetorical, I did not answer. Hedke said he was not responsible for the photo appearing on Facebook but he didn't seem to regret the aftermath. "Linda, we are in a battle for our lives in this country. You have to trust me on this. You can already see it unfolding in France and in Britain, where Islamic growth is faster, heads and shoulders, than any other religions," he told me, his blue eyes peering at me through black-rimmed glasses. "It matters what we teach our kids in school. We are learning the hard way, in my opinion."

"Do you consider this indoctrination?" I asked.

"Absolutely," he said. "Our system is just being substantially in-doctrinated on that subject matter."

At the central office's request and largely because of Hedke's pro-tests, Hope was asked to give a group of lawmakers a tour of the school. Hedke was a no-show. He could not make it because of a prior engagement. Hope showed the lawmakers the school, pointed out the painting of the Last Supper, took them to a classroom where there was some discussion about Christianity as part of a history lesson, and explained the curriculum. Hope, a Core Knowledge neophyte before she came to Minneha, had become a strong advo-cate. She realized that naysayers needed what Minneha's teachers provided students: a basic education about major world religions.

During the hubbub, no Muslims from the school had spoken up. Suad Attaria, who had a son in kindergarten and a daughter in fourth grade at Minneha, was shocked and offended when the teachers removed the bulletin-board display about Islam. But she decided not to complain because she did not want to stir up more trouble. She could not understand, though, why anyone would re-act so strongly to an educational display on Islam or find a bulletin board threatening. The school, she said, had agreed to teach about Islam more than a decade ago and should not bow down to one person's opinion. She taught math and English as a second language at a private Islamic school in Wichita. She hurt for her children as outsiders piled on hate toward Muslims and Minneha. She had liked that her children and their peers learned about other faiths, a lesson she had seen as desperately needed since moving to Wichita from the Palestinian territories eleven years before. As we spoke in the family's home in an upscale Wichita subdivision, Attaria wore a hijab and a long dress. She had come to America after marrying Kamal, who had first come to the United States in 1977 to attend college. He became an industrial engineer and works in flight testing at Bombardier. He didn't think it was right that Minneha took down the sign but understood that the school just could not stand up to the radical right. He and his wife had sensed anti-Muslim sentiment building not just in the aftermath of 9/11 but in the wake of the Boston Marathon bombings.[28]

About six months before, just weeks after the Boston Marathon bombings, Attaria had taken a walk in sweatpants and her hijab. When she strolled from her subdivision to the next, some men working on a house shouted at her, "Jihad." She was so scared that she ran back home. She also felt the stares of strangers while shopping for groceries at the nearby Dillons. For a while she stopped going to the grocery store at night, said the soft-spoken Attaria, who offered me baklava and tea from a Palestinian tea set in the family's high-ceilinged living room. Their home had signs of the family's pride in their faith: the family Koran in a wooden box decorated by Palestinian embroidery, the framed picture on the fireplace mantel with Koranic verses, including one meant to protect them from Satan and another that stated a core belief, that Muslims should believe only in Allah.

The Attarias' eldest child, Salsabila, wore a hijab only when she entered a mosque. At home where I met her, she had her long, black hair tied back in a ponytail and wore shorts and a T-shirt with the slogan "Peace and Love." School, she said, generally had been a safe place for her. She heard only an occasional slam on her religion, like the previous month when a peer made fun of her mother and said wearing a hijab was disgusting. Salsabila wanted to lash out verbally at the student, but her mother urged her daughter not to overreact. "Do we want to please Allah our God or do we want to be offended by a ten-year-old who doesn't know that much about it?" she asked her.

The mother supported the effort to teach about other religions, but had been unhappy at times with the way a teacher presented Islam. In the first grade, Salsabila came home with a chart that listed various things about different religions. For important people, in the Islam box, the chart listed Mohammed and Allah. Attaria complained to the school that that was incorrect. "I said, 'Allah is not a person. Allah is God.'" The teacher said she would review the information. The Attarias do not know if the information was changed for future lessons. I looked at a Core Knowledge chart for the first graders, and it listed only Mohammed as a key figure under Islam. Regardless, the chart Salsabila took home did not sour her parents on the religions unit. Her mother spoke to the first-grade class about Islam at the teacher's request and talked about the five pillars. She brought homemade Middle Eastern pastries made from dates, showed the family's Koran, and demonstrated the movements Muslims use in prayer. The children followed up with many questions. She taught them, too, how Muslims greeted one another, saying, "Peace be upon you," in Arabic. Attaria thought Core Knowledge would make a difference because the lessons exposed such young children to the fact that Muslims exist, they live in the same city, and they attend the same school.

The message gets through, if my conversations with fifth graders were any indication. I met with small groups of them in a conference room. Many were well aware of the bulletin-board controversy because for weeks they'd had to walk by several security guards on their way into the school. Tracy Nguyen's mother is Christian and her father is Buddhist, and both of the eleven-year-old's parents are from Vietnam. Tracy told me she thought the uproar was ridiculous. Then speaking quickly, she let out a torrent of words she had been wanting to say for a long time: "It's a bulletin board, and children should have the right to learn about other stuff instead of their own religion because there are more things in life than just their own religion." Before she studied the different religions, she did not know anything about Islam. Now she knew more about Muslim practices and holidays. She knew some of the religious and cultural reasons for wearing a hijab. Their teachers, Tracy and other students said, taught them to understand that religions had similarities and differences, and that was okay with them. That was okay, some students told me, even if their parents did not think the same way.

The Karps told me they never meant for their complaint to cause issues for Minneha. Liz Karp, who objected to the use of the term "five pillars," was fine with a display on Islamic art. But she still would have preferred that her son's teachers not include religion as part of the curriculum. Religion, she said, was confusing, complex, and extremely personal. Just how, she wondered, are they going to teach it to children this young? It didn't make sense to her to even try.

Fed up with the negative comments by critics who had never observed the classes, Minneha's principal agreed to let me see the program for myself. I was particularly interested in first grade because it was the earliest Minneha students learn about religion. The principal led me to Fagg, who had won accolades for her fidelity to the Core Knowledge curriculum. Fagg used the program's suggested read-aloud stories for first graders on the religions and a set of provided first-grade texts called *Three World Religions.* She also added props to the lessons, and she clued in her students about how she found some of the extra materials and how she was learning along with them.

I watched Fagg's class for three days in a row, getting a peek at the first set of lessons about the world's religions. My son at the time was in kindergarten but I could easily see him sitting among the children as Fagg told her first graders about her recent find: "So, one day, it was my second year at Minneha, and I thought, 'Wouldn't it be neat to find a menorah?' It was one day after the Christmas holiday season, and I happened to be in Target, and they had this reduced merchandise, and I went over and started looking through it, and guess what I got?" she said in a chipper tone. Then she reached to her windowsill to get the menorah. I doubted my son would have oohed at the sight like the Wichita children had done. He had seen menorahs many times but he likely would have been proud that a teacher was showing the students something about Judaism. Fagg, who told me to call her Debbie, treated each fact, each image about a religion as something exciting, something new, something real the children could see. They started the unit on the three world religions with a little review.

Previously, they had learned about polytheism, and "poly" means what, the teacher asked? "Many," the children recited. "Many gods."

"'Monotheistic' means how many gods?"

"One," answered the children, who sat on the classroom rug facing Fagg, stationed in a chair next to a small bulletin board with a list of vocabulary words for the morning, including Christianity, Judaism, Islam, faithful, shrine, and religion. She read from the Core Knowledge program's book for first-grade teachers but often broke from the script to gauge what knowledge the children already had. She asked the children to name religious groups. "Muslim," one child offered. "Hindu," another said.

"Sharks," a third said.

I avoided chuckling and so did Fagg, who kept a straight face as she commented, "That wouldn't be a religion. That would be an animal, okay."

She taught them simple definitions. Islam was the religion of Muslims. A shrine was a sacred place. The children struggled to pronounce some of the words, including Christianity, and practiced how to say them with Fagg. "Okay, crisscross applesauce, and we are ready for an awesome history lesson today," announced their teacher, who asked them to turn and face the classroom Smart Board, where she then showed a picture-laden PowerPoint presentation about the three world religions. It was a lesson on facts but also an attempt to explain the inexplicable, what religion was and why it came to be.

"Have you ever wondered how the universe came to be?" Fagg asked in a voice tinged with a sense of mystery. Several of the children answered, "Yeah!" "Or why the stars shine at night? Or what makes a rainbow?" she asked. Yes, yes, the children responded. "Well, you are not alone," Fagg said, eyeing the text through her dark-colored glasses. "Lots of people have wondered about these same things for thousands of years." So far, so good. I liked that Fagg adhered to Core Knowledge's philosophy: teach about religion as a part of history. Don't make judgments.

In the search for answers, many people began following religions, she told the children. "Religion refers to the belief and worship in a superhuman power," she said. Maybe schools that use this curriculum should have parent visitation days so parents will better understand how religion is handled and can be handled as an academic subject. Fagg was open about her Catholic faith in conversations but showed no bias toward Christianity as she taught. She showed a slide of three houses of worship depicted in bright colors: a synagogue, a church, and a mosque. The children learned the names of each institution and the symbols that distinguished them: A cross for Christianity. A Star of David for Judaism. A crescent and star for Islam. Then she took them on a photographic tour of places of worship in Jerusalem: the Western Wall, the Church of the Holy Sepulchre, and the golden Dome of the Rock.

Our family had traveled to Israel during the spring of 2014, when my son was in kindergarten. At my urging, we visited all three of those sites. It was only about three months before the conflict between Israel and Hamas escalated into war in Gaza. We were allowed to tour the grounds of the Temple Mount and hired a Muslim guide. Our son, by then six and a bit travel weary, tuned in and out of the guide's narration. He was quick, though, to reach out and touch the marble of the Dome of the Rock when the guide said that was okay. He marveled at the shine of the golden dome and the colorful geometric design below it. They were images that I hoped would remain with him as he grew, just like the photos Fagg had shown her students.

The next day, I was there as Fagg began the lessons on Judaism. She first taught them vocabulary words, such as *prophet, Jew, synagogue, Jewish,* and *Hebrew*. She nudged the students to turn their attention from her to a Smart Board as she began the slide show on Judaism. A photo of a young girl appeared early. "Hi, I'm Miriam. I'm a Jew," Fagg read, and Miriam became the children's guide as they learned about Judaism, its history, its holy book known as the Torah, and its holidays. Volunteers rolled up paper to mimic the scrolls of a Torah. The children saw Miriam's synagogue in Jerusalem and counted the points in the Star of David. Fagg read about Passover, acting as if she were Miriam. "Would you like to join my family at our Seder?" she asked, pronouncing the word "*see*-der" rather than with the Hebrew pronunciation "*say*-der."

Sitting a few feet away, I couldn't help but whisper the correct pronunciation. The teacher repeated it, then stumbled again over Rosh Hashanah. She looked to me for guidance and I helped, now feeling chagrined that I had interrupted. She later said she did not mind. She wanted to get the words right. The teacher did the best she could to follow the pronunciation laid out in the Core Knowledge books. Fagg was fine in accepting children's corrections if they happened to celebrate the holidays she did not know as well. But as a parent, I didn't like that a teacher would rely on young children for correct pronunciations. My son went to religious school at our temple but he was not yet an expert on pronouncing the names of Jewish holidays. He was just learning them himself. I quizzed the Wichita schools superintendent on that point. He was not concerned that a teacher did not know how to pronounce all of the religious terms correctly. He saw nothing wrong with children raising their hands and correcting their teachers. Teachers, he said, were not infallible.[29]

As Fagg finished the slide show, a girl waved her hand in the air and the teacher called on her. "All the Jewish people have banks because they have money," the girl said. The teacher looked uncomfortable but quickly moved on with the lesson with barely any comment. I winced when I heard the girl's remark and hated to see the teacher miss an opportunity to talk about negative stereotypes. I spoke with Fagg about it after class, and she told me she did not say anything because she was concerned about stepping on parents' toes. She also felt that her students learned about respect each month as part of lessons on different character traits. They recited mantras about how it was important to be respectful to others, to be tolerant of differences. Her response did not reassure me. If this comment had been made in my son's class, I would have been livid that the teacher let it go without a word. It was a perfect moment to correct an inappropriate remark and teach a broader lesson to the class about avoiding stereotypes. If an adult said those same words about Jews, it would be called prejudice. I did not hold it against Fagg. After spending almost a week in her classroom, I knew Fagg was a teacher really trying to get it right. She, like her colleagues, had received no training that dealt specifically with religion. No one had advised her how to respond to some of the things children might say, coincidentally the very concern that some parents at Minneha had had.

Angelique Badgett, a second-grade teacher who came to Minneha when Core Knowledge was introduced there, became my sounding board at the school. She wanted to teach at Minneha because she was a fan of Hirsch, whose philosophy includes mixing art and music with other classroom content. Badgett saw the approach as a way to excite students about history. She studied weaving in a fine arts program before going to graduate school for education, and, as a teacher, she worked hard to teach second graders concepts using art. She had them do an art project with white and black blocks and gray in between to try to teach them that our society was filled with gray. A Methodist from Virginia, she described herself as fairly liberal. She thought it was important to teach about other religions even if teachers and parents weren't comfortable with it. Teachers and parents both needed to make their children understand that it was okay to be a Muslim, Jew, Hindu, Christian, or, for that matter, anything, she told me.[30] We spoke at first during one of her breaks in her classroom, which she had filled with books about Buddhism and Hinduism, then continued the conversation by phone when we ran out of time. She'd known nothing about Hinduism so educated herself, a responsibility she thought all teachers should assume. She agreed, though, with the superintendent that society could not expect teachers to know how to pronounce everything.

On other aspects of teaching about religion, Badgett saw no gray. Holidays should be discussed only when they come up in the curriculum. Teachers needed to respect the fact that not all children marked the same holidays and recognize that school was the place to learn about the culture and history of religions, not celebrate particular holidays. Families could celebrate holidays at home. I mentioned the comment the first grader had made about bankers in Fagg's class. There are always children who will repeat stereotypes about race and religion in the classroom, and teachers should not be shy about reacting, she said. Had a child made a comment about Jews and bankers, Badgett said she would have responded with a simple lesson about stereotypes. She would have told children that some people believed that, but it was not really true, and that that kind of statement was what we called a stereotype. She would have added that there were many Jews who are not bankers. There were Jewish teachers, lawyers, doctors, and workers at McDonald's or the mall. She was well aware, too, that if she gave that response, she might make at least one child's parents unhappy. She was willing to face the consequences. To Badgett, a teacher's job was to open children's minds, not keep them closed. Her reaction to the opposition over the Islam display on a bulletin board: "You've got to be kidding me."

—⁂—

Because of the bulletin-board flap, many Minneha teachers, including Fagg, began doing more to inform parents about the upcoming lessons on religion. In the past, Fagg had mentioned the unit in her weekly newsletter, but in the fall of 2013 she talked about it in person with each student's parents at parent-teacher conferences. She explained what they were doing and what was coming up. She told them she was not teaching religion. She was teaching history. The controversy roiled the school, but maybe it had served a good purpose, Fagg said. She realized the importance of keeping parents in the loop.

Watching Fagg's class on the third day of the world religions unit, I had no problems grasping how teachers could teach about religion to six- and seven-year-olds. This time, she was giving the lesson on Christianity. She taught vocabulary related to the religion, mentioning how they would hear the word "miracle" in the reading. What might make a miracle happen, she asked? "Jesus," a boy said.

"Ooh, Jesus might make it happen?" she repeated, not judging the boy's answer.

"A miracle, in Christianity, what the Christians believe is, it is something that happens unexpectedly, out of the ordinary, and they think it happened because of God," she said.

"Okay, put your eyes on me again. You're going to be listening to find out who Christians believe Jesus Christ to be," she said and began a story using the narrator, Peter, a Christian boy from Jerusalem. "In fact, Jesus was a Jew," she read as a slide appeared of Jesus as a baby with Mary and Joseph. "Who's that baby in the swaddling blankets?" she asked. "Jesus," many of the children said. Fagg went on, reading verbatim from the Core Knowledge text to explain who Jesus was: "Jesus was a holy leader and a special teacher. Christians today believe Jesus is the Messiah, sent to save the people here on earth. Christians also believe that Jesus is the son of God." Through Peter, the children learned about Easter and Christmas in as neutral a way as possible. Those two Christian holidays have been somewhat of a mystery to my own son because he views them through a commercial lens, having never heard much about the religious aspects. Ask him what Easter is, and I suspect my son would talk about chocolate bunnies. Christmas, to him, has meant colorful lights and Santa Claus, whom he wished would bring him presents even though his family did not celebrate the holiday. I would have been fine with him hearing Fagg's lessons that day.

As hands-on projects, the first graders attached two colored triangles to make a Star of David to represent a Jewish symbol. For Christianity they made a cross, and for Islam they cut out a crescent and star. A Muslim fifth grader I spoke with during my visit to Minneha had told me how he objected to making a cross so his teacher let him make only the symbol for Islam instead. Benjamin Karp also had shied away from activities involving religions that were not his own. Later, maybe both boys will realize the gift that their school tried to give them at a young age. They did not have to duck their heads in shame. Their school made it possible to talk about faith with pride, whether a child was Christian, Muslim, Hindu, Buddhist, or Jewish. It did not, for the most part, try to force one particular religion on them. If only mine had done the same.

CHAPTER FIVE

The Church Lady

THE DAY Jesus Christ entered my fourth-grade classroom, my childhood forever changed.

It was 1974 and my family had just moved from western New York State to rural Ohio. I was the new kid. All I wanted was to fit in. But one afternoon that first week, a slender woman in a long skirt walked into my class and my regular teacher walked out, leaving this stranger in charge. The woman stuck figures of Jesus Christ and other bearded figures on a flannel board. In a soft tone, she told a story about how Jesus had solved the problems of the people visiting him.

Twisting the ends of my dark-blonde ponytail, I listened in confusion. I could not understand why she was in my class talking about Jesus. I wanted to crawl underneath the wooden desk and disappear. Now, the class visitor was asking us to talk about Jesus and his effect on our lives. Some of my classmates waved their hands in the air, eager to answer. My discomfort grew. So did my embarrassment that all of this was so foreign to me.

"Let's sing," the woman said. Around me, the woman and my classmates started singing:

"Jesus loves me, this I know, for the Bible tells me so . . ."

I kept my lips pursed shut. I had never sung that song before. I had never even heard it. I could have easily picked up the words of the refrain, but did not want to try. I was Jewish. I did not believe in Jesus. The class visitor, I learned later, taught weekly Bible classes in all elementary classrooms. She was one of several religious education teachers who visited elementary schools across Hancock County to teach Bible stories and songs about Jesus. An organization supported by area Protestant churches paid the teachers. My middle brother, Kevin, a sixth grader, and I both received visits from the Bible class instructor our first week in our new school. My eldest brother, as a high school freshman, was spared from the Christianity classes. The Van Buren school system was located on a patch of land at the crest of a rare hill in northwest Ohio and drew fewer than a thousand students from Van Buren, a one-stoplight town of just two hundred, and from a few nearby towns. The students were a mix, the children of farmers, retail clerks, and educated professionals who worked at Marathon Oil, Cooper Tire, or Findlay College. But it was the religiosity that was the area's most notable feature. I dubbed my class visitor the Church Lady. All through childhood, I never knew her name.

After school on the day the Church Lady came, my brothers and I ran off the school bus into our family's one-story brick ranch in a subdivision of mostly cookie-cutter homes. Kevin and I pushed the yellow vinyl bar stools close to the kitchen counter and fumed to our mother. We were adamant. We did not want to sit in those religion classes again. My mother's face flushed in anger. Not only should we not have to sit in those classes, she said, but Van Buren should not be running them. It was illegal, a violation of the US Constitution's First Amendment. My parents protested to the schools superintendent, who told them he didn't want to make waves. Yet, he agreed to speak to the school board. My mother urged him to do it privately. "I don't want my children hurt," she said.[1]

The superintendent spoke to the school board but it refused to eliminate the classes. My brother and I could be excused, the superintendent said. My parents debated whether to take legal action, then vetoed the idea out of fear of retaliation. That same week, the local branch of the KKK burned a cross on the yard of one of the few black families living in Findlay. At first, my fourth-grade teacher sat with me in another room when I was excused from the religion classes. Then, one day she ushered me into a room the size of a broom closet and told me to stay there until she returned. The room smelled of chalk. Mom called the school to complain, and the teacher agreed to send me to the library but damage had been done. I felt my classmates' eyes follow me as I left the classroom and the Church Lady entered. It was hard enough being the new kid. Now, I was subject to regular interrogations by some of my peers.

"Why can't you sit in the class with us?" a classmate asked one day.

"I'm Jewish," I said.

"What do you mean, 'You're Jewish'?"

I was not sure how to answer. I was in elementary school just learning about my religion in Hebrew school. Our family never went to temple for services and God did not come up in conversation. We did a few of the basics of Judaism—dipping apples in honey to mark the start of Rosh Hashanah, the Jewish New Year, and lighting candles at Hanukkah before having a present orgy just like many of our Christian friends had at Christmas. At Van Buren we were the odd ones out because we did not accept Jesus as our savior. Christianity was a part of our school system's fabric, stitched into numerous parts of the school day. Every day, a youth minister roved the cafeteria chatting with students and inviting them to Christian youth club events. The Church Lady taught only in the elementary school grades, but at Easter and Christmas the school hosted assemblies for all grades at which pastors led us in prayer, always ending with, "In Jesus's name, I pray." By age twelve, I persuaded my parents to let me quit Hebrew school. The nearly hour-long drive each Sunday was wearing and I wasn't connecting much with other children at the temple. I felt like an outsider even among Jews. The longer I went to Van Buren, the less I saw to like about any religion.

"Do you believe in Jesus?" a high school teammate asked as I gave her a ride home from basketball practice.

"No," I said, "I'm Jewish."

"You'll go to hell then, won't you?" she said.

I shook my head no, then tried to focus on keeping my Honda Civic moving straight ahead on the single-lane country road. I had no pat answer and wanted to change the conversation's direction as she asked more questions about Jews and the afterlife. When it came to life and death, I knew more about what Jews did not believe than what they did.

"You'll end up in hell," my teammate said.

I wasn't a spiritual Jew in childhood. I was mostly a book Jew, learning bits about my religion's history through the words of other Jews. I was fascinated by *My Life*, the autobiography of Golda Meir, Israel's prime minister from 1969 to 1974. She, like my maternal grandfather and great-grandparents, was born in Russia, and the pogroms drove her family away to America during her childhood. She recalled what it was like watching her father and a neighbor barricade their homes with boards to thwart a pogrom, a riot meant to lead to the massacre of Jews. "And above all, I remember being aware that this was happening to me because I was Jewish, which made me different from most of the other children in the yard. It was a feeling that I was to know again many times during my life—the fear, the frustration, the consciousness of being different and the profound instinctive belief that if one wanted to survive, one had to take effective action personally."[2]

Fear, frustration, survival. Those words stuck with me as I created a jaded definition of what it meant to be a Jew. To be a Jew: hover on society's sidelines, trying to blend in yet constantly being pushed away. To be a Jew: be different and alone. To be a Jew in a town where there were almost none: live in apprehension of what someone might do or say.

"You Jewish son of a bitch," a boy taunted Kevin on the school bus during his junior year and my freshman year of high school.

I heard the epithet and flinched. Kevin grimaced but let the taunt go. He and some neighborhood boys had disagreed over something. A few days later, on a Saturday morning, we woke to discover anti-Semitic graffiti on nearly every window of our house. The same graffiti, a swastika, was etched in white wax on the windows of Kevin's lime-green Barracuda in the driveway. Our family did not make a police report but Kevin called a deputy sheriff he had become friends with through scouting. The deputy visited the homes of the young suspects, but no one confessed. For several mornings on our school bus ride past acres of wheat and soy bean fields, we heard whispers about the marks left on our windows. I was angry and puzzled. What fueled such venom? Was it anti-Semitism or was it ignorance? In Findlay, when we moved there, there were only two or three Jewish families. The closest temples, in Toledo and Lima, were nearly an hour's drive away and our town had no visible Jewish presence. No one asked my family to bring in a menorah to the schools and talk about Hanukkah. Nor did we make that offer. We did not want to make ourselves stand out more.

Our high school teachers had opportunities to teach us about other religions in an academic way but did not. When it was time to teach about the Holocaust in my American history class in the late 1970s, my teacher read a few paragraphs from the textbook. About twenty-five of us sat in horizontal rows of desks scribbling as fast as we could in our notebooks. The teacher, a fiftysomething man with thinning gray hair and round glasses, spoke about the Holocaust as if it were something that had happened hundreds of years ago. With his monotone voice, he could have been reading a passage in a science book about a colony of ants when he read how six million Jews were killed in the Holocaust. The boy behind me, a muscular, curly, blond-haired teen, leaned forward and whispered in my ear in a hoarse, low voice: "Kike. My grandfather was in the KKK." I said nothing and refused to look at him, unwilling to give him the satisfaction of knowing his comment had hurt so much that my stomach clenched in pain. I didn't know this boy well. He was on the school wrestling team and occasionally tried to cheat off me during quizzes. I was part of the college-prep crowd; he was not. My teacher did not hear the slur and I did not report the incident. Whom could I trust when everyone seemingly supported preaching in the classroom and religious assemblies?

Before I graduated from high school in 1982, I made a plea to my principal. A minister led us in prayer and invoked the name of Jesus at my brothers' graduations. Could the school ask the minister to give only a nonsectarian prayer at my graduation? Please, I said, keep Jesus out of it. My principal agreed, but the message apparently did not make its way to the prayer leader, the youth minister who sat with students at lunchtime. He asked us to bow our heads, said a prayer, and ended by asking us all to pray in Jesus's name. Once again, I felt like that little girl who wanted to sink into the floor the day the Church Lady came to class. I felt like an outcast.

I never should have had to deal with the Church Lady, but I had no idea about the history of such classes until I recently began researching church/state court battles in our country. In 1948, the Supreme Court ruled 8–1 in *McCollum v. Board of Education* that holding weekly religious education classes inside public schools was unconstitutional. The plaintiff, Vashti McCollum, an atheist, sued the Champaign, Illinois, schools on behalf of her three sons. But it was her eldest son Jim's experiences that motivated her the most. In 1944, when he was in fifth grade, he was told to sit in the hall when he was excused from attending the religion classes; the hall was the same place kids were sent for punishment. He came home in tears. Jim was teased and bullied in school and often beaten up on the way home.[3] His family was the one who sued, but others suffered at the same time. Jim remembered a classmate who was "outed" as Jewish because he too did not attend those classes. The boy was beaten and his glasses were broken.[4] I bit back tears as I read this history. The ruling in favor of the McCollums happened twenty-five years before my Church Lady encounter.

During childhood, I indirectly blamed the Church Lady for the isolation and ostracism I experienced and more directly blamed some of my peers for the way they treated me and my brothers. But was it really the fault of children? My peers knew little about my faith. I knew more about theirs because of exposure yet I couldn't have made the points I know so well now. I probably was not that sensitive or respectful of some of my peers' faith because of my ignorance. I couldn't have pointed out to them that because Christianity grew out of Judaism we were being raised with many of the same values. Where we differed the most was our view of Jesus. He was their savior. He was not mine. But it did not have to be a difference that divided us. In the spring of 2013 I traveled to Van Buren in search of answers. I had returned only a few times since high school because my parents had moved in 1988. Was the Church Lady still teaching those classes? Was my school doing anything to expose students to other religions or did the community's Christian influence still trump everything?

First, I was determined to find the Church Lady but I didn't even know her name. I called the county board of education hoping for a lead and lucked out. The administrative assistant who answered the phone, Ruthann Walters, had taught those Bible classes, too, though not at Van Buren. She offered to call around to find out who taught the Van Buren classes. She was eager to help. For years, Walters had carried some guilt about teaching those classes. She had begun teaching them, once a week for fifteen minutes, in 1977. Walters began having doubts as opposition to the classes grew in Findlay, the largest of the county's school systems. In 1979 several people threatened to sue if the program wasn't removed during the school day. The school system responded by moving the program to before and after school. Then, in January 1984, two years after my high school graduation, a Unitarian minister, Lawrence A. F. Ford, and his wife,

Polly Millet, sued the Findlay schools, asking the courts to rule that public school classrooms could not be used for religious education classes even if the classes were held before or after school hours. The lawsuit claimed that holding the program in elementary schools so close to start and dismissal times gave the impression that the school system was endorsing religious instruction. School personnel, the suit said, also had distributed materials about the program, including flyers that proclaimed that in the weekly classes, "Children learn about God, Jesus, the world and how to understand and get along with others! The Bible is used as the resource on moral and personal values."[5] Homeroom teachers collected registration and permission slips for the program. After the suit's initial filing, the school system stopped allowing staff to distribute materials. In August 1985 a federal judge ruled in favor of the plaintiffs, supporting their reasoning that a program designed for eight- and nine-year-olds was directed at too impressionable an age group. The children, the judge agreed, were too young to understand that an outside group, not their school, was promoting Christianity as an afterschool activity.[6]

Walters read about how the Findlay program made non-Christian children uncomfortable and questioned her role even though she loved teaching the classes. She shooed away an assistant as we talked in a conference room at the county's board of education. This sixty-eight-year-old woman with thinning, reddish-blonde hair and wisps of bangs framing her pale face had an air of fragility but also a spirit that sparkled like the glitter on her rose-and-brown sweater. She clearly wanted to talk. She recalled barely noticing the few kids who slipped discreetly away each time she came into the classroom to teach the Bible class.[7] Those children had been excused for reasons she never knew. Tears came to her eyes as she spoke about the decision to no longer teach the classes. She had started to wonder if her presence was affecting the kids who did not stay. Her voice cracking, she described how seeing children walk out broke her heart. She began to wonder if she was making them feel different. Walters was a young mother in her twenties when she taught those classes. She did not have a teaching degree, though she had always dreamed of being a full-time teacher. The daughter of farmers, she couldn't afford college. Teaching the Bible classes was a mission for her, a mission to teach Christian values. But that quest lost its luster after the Findlay controversy. That I had been one of those children who had to leave the room particularly bothered Walters, who greeted me with a big smile, as if she had known me for years. There was a chance our paths had crossed decades earlier. Her twin daughters were born the same year as I, and it turned out we played against each other on rival basketball teams as our parents cheered for us in the stands. Walters over time developed a less Christian-centric view of the world. She stopped thinking it was okay to teach those religion classes.

The main plaintiff in that 1984 case, Richard A. F. Ford, would become the most hated man in Findlay for fighting to end such a locally prized institution. Ford, whose stepchildren attended Findlay schools, received threats,[8] and leaders of area churches and other supporters held a rally in favor of the weekday religious education programs. The woman I had dubbed the Church Lady was there. I know because she told me. Walters had helped me locate the woman. Her name was Dorothy Powell, and in 2013 she was one of two teachers still teaching weekly religion classes at four school systems in the county. Van Buren no longer offered the classes. In the remaining school systems, Powell and another teacher taught the class at nearby churches during the school day. Children were bused to the church or walked there depending on the distance from their school. Powell now taught classes to children in grades 1 through 5 in Arlington, a school system about the size of Van Buren, similarly situated off a country road. The Church Lady was the symbol of so much of my childhood angst. Powell, though, had no idea of any of that.

Now seventy-eight, the five-foot, six-inch Powell was hunched over because of age. Her cheeks, framed by brown-and-gray coiffed hair, were a tad rosy and slightly wrinkled. She looked every bit the grandmother of nine she had become. She had long ago relinquished the skirts she used to wear in favor of pants and black, ballet-slipper-style shoes. She had received some Bible training in college, which she dropped out of after one year to marry. While Walters saw the 1984 case as a reason to end the weekly Bible classes for public school students, Powell did not. She remained as committed to the effort as she had been when she started teaching the classes in the mid-1960s. Her husband, in fact, had been president of the Hancock County Religious Education Association for roughly fifty years. Like him, Powell always believed in the program's original goal: to reach unchurched families.[9] A retired Methodist minister from the area founded the group in 1944 because he realized many elementary students in the county did not attend church so probably didn't get a chance to hear the stories of the Bible.[10] The program teaches values that the children dearly need, values that they don't get from the television shows they watch, Powell said. When the Ford case erupted in Findlay, Powell and the other religious education teachers stopped their classes in area schools for about six months. Powell stopped teaching at Van Buren entirely a few years later because a parent threatened to sue the school system if it didn't remove the program.

As we talked, Powell and I sat across from each other in a classroom at Good Hope Lutheran Church in Arlington before her classes started for the day. Through the window, I could see the brick front of the Arlington school building. I asked if she ever thought about the children who were excused from her class over the years.

"Some of them were of a faith that didn't want anyone else to teach them differently," she said.

"How did you feel about them?"

"They weren't treated badly," she said, her voice retaining the gentle tone she used from the moment we met.

"How do you know?" I asked.

"Well, I don't know," she said.

"I'm going to tell you a little story, okay?" I said, trying to keep my voice from cracking. It felt as if I were about to give a confession. I rambled on about how I was Jewish and my family had moved to Van Buren from upstate New York. I didn't know what I expected as I told her how I felt the day she came into my classroom. "Now imagine," I said, "I'm Jewish. We do not believe in Jesus. We are not Christians. And there she was, this lady in a skirt with a felt board and felt figures telling all of us to sing, 'Jesus loves me.' And I sat there in that room, and you know what I wanted to do?" I said, my voice still shaky. "Sink down to the floor as low as I possibly could."

She seemed at a loss as she searched for a response. At first she just said, "Oh." Then she recalled how there was a Jewish boy who loved the class until she started teaching about the New Testament. I mentioned that I had two older brothers, one of whom would have been in sixth grade at the time and the other in high school, too old for the religion classes given only in elementary grades. I didn't tell her that my brother Kevin had expressed distaste for her class right away. He also thought religious school at our temple was boring.

She asked me if any of the children made fun of me because I was Jewish. I responded that they did, from 1974 to 1982, the whole time I was at Van Buren.

"Really?" she asked.

I nodded, but afterward I wished I had amplified. It wasn't as if every student accosted me about my religion. I had had friends through playing flute in the band, competing on the basketball team, running track, and working on the yearbook. But the Church Lady's visit to my classroom singled me out in front of peers, and some never forgot that I was different in a school with no visible diversity.

Powell told me she was sorry I had experienced that, yet she did not link what had happened to her presence in the school. Most Christians, she said, feel a kinship for the Jews because so much of the Christian faith stems from the Old Testament. She described how she taught the children good Christian values and those included respecting others regardless of their faith. Unlike Walters, Powell did not see herself as part of the problem.

Yet she told me she knew that offering the classes inside the school during the school day was not legal. She taught them anyway because school boards in the various county towns supported the program. I questioned whether teaching the class off school grounds during the school day was legal, and she said it was. Surprised, I checked. She was right. In 1952, in *Zorach v. Clauson*, the Supreme Court ruled that schools could release students during school hours to go to religious centers for instruction or devotional exercises as long as the schools did not promote the classes. It was the court's way of compromising on behalf of religious leaders who wanted assurances that schools were not acting hostilely toward religion.[11] Dissenting justices noted that the ruling created the same problem that in-classroom programs had: students would be divided into two groups, those who went to the religion classes and those who did not.[12]

Release time has long been a fixture across the country, particularly in Utah, where Mormons built seminaries next to schools so students could easily walk over for religious instruction during the day. The longtime friends I stayed with during my 2013 visit to Van Buren coincidentally had moved back to the area in 2003 from Salt Lake City. My friends, one of whom grew up Catholic and the other of whom belonged to the Church of God, an evangelical Christian branch, left Utah partly because of the influence of the Mormon church on the public schools. They worried, in particular, about the release-time program, which began in high school. So they moved before their eldest child entered high school. The majority of students at the high school regularly left for one class period to attend classes on scripture in the Mormon seminary at the end of the parking lot. The program, run by the Church of Jesus Christ of Latter-day Saints, was voluntary, but my friends believed their son would have felt pushed to go.

Very few students opted out of the classes Powell now taught. As we talked, she motioned to me to follow her to a bigger class-room so she could set up for her first class. She stuck an easel in the middle of the room and rested on it a flannel board, similar to the one I had seen four decades before. It's called a flannel graph, and teachers have used it for years as a teaching aid during Bible classes. A little after noon, a parent volunteer walked in, leading about twenty third graders. About twenty more from another class soon joined them, and Powell led them in a Christian song called "The Butterfly Song," written by Brian M. Howard. The children nearly shouted the last line of the refrain, which thanked God for making them.[13] As the children and their teacher sang, light streamed in on them through a big window that faced their school. They went from songs to Bible stories. The parent volunteer escorted the group out, and another class, seventeen second graders, shuffled in. Powell led them in a different song and then began telling a story about how Jesus healed a very ill man. She used six-inch-tall characters, including Jesus, on the flannel board.

There was this man who couldn't walk, though he had family and friends who cared for him, she began. "Could you imagine never having been able to walk and not having anything to help him like we have now?" she asked the children. She showed the man's friends carrying him out the door and down the street to a house where Jesus was holding court with his followers. She tapped a foot on the floor to make the sound of the friends making a hole in the house's roof. They lowered the ill man into the room in front of Jesus, who just looked at the man, smiled, and told him he was forgiven. Then Jesus said to stand up and walk, Powell narrated. The man stood up. He was made well, making it a very special day. "His friends," she said, "had faith that Jesus could make him well." She looked at her young listeners. "When Jesus does something that only he and God could do, there is a word for it," she said, then provided the answer. "It's called a miracle." She was a mesmerizing storyteller. Her class was perfect for religious school. But for me it really brought home why it was so important to push instruction about the world's religions to lower grades: to show the diversity of religions as well as similarities, rather than preach that one faith is the answer. There was a difference between Powell's description of a miracle, for example, and the way the Wichita first-grade teacher had explained miracles to her students. Powell made it seem as if the power of Jesus to make miracles was an accepted fact. Wichita's Debbie Fagg carefully measured her words, noting it was something Christians believed.

After the second class, I got up to leave and Powell walked over. She said she was thinking about our earlier conversation and wanted me to know she was sorry that other children had treated me badly. She told me she makes a point to tell her students that Jews are God's chosen people when the class talks about the Old Testament. Good Christians, she said, looked at Judaism as the beginning of Christianity. I smiled and nodded, unsure of how to respond. I never wanted my peers in elementary school to look at me as if I were one of God's chosen people. I wanted them to see me as one of them, not an "other." I asked Powell what she thought of a public school class about different religions and described what I saw in the sixth-grade class in Wellesley. She said she wouldn't object to such a high school course but wasn't sure about middle school. It would depend on the sixth grader's maturity.

"I think it would be good if kids could learn about other religions," I said.

She paused. "Well, yes, I'm not sure. I'm not sure about the Muslims. The Jews, they came to this country, and they didn't try to change things. They sort of did their own thing. The Muslims, I think they're trying to change what other people do."

A few weeks later, I was with my family watching a rehearsal of the reenactment of the Revolutionary War's Battle of Lexington on the Battle Green when my cell phone rang. It was Powell. Her voice was friendly, and I responded with niceties. But, inwardly, I panicked. Did she regret speaking with me? I asked if I could call back later. Rounds of fake but deafening musket shots were about to go off. Later, sitting in my car in a nearby parking lot, I called back. She wanted to apologize again for what I had experienced. Since I had left her that day at the church in Arlington, she had been thinking. It bothered her that children she taught were unkind to me because I was Jewish. She reiterated how she taught the older children about Israel and how Jews were special as a result.[14] I cringed to again hear her describe Jews that way. Yet I could no longer hold any bitterness toward the Church Lady. Her perspective was based on her experiences. She, like many of my peers, could not have known how I felt about those weekly religion classes or about the interrogations I experienced afterward. The cause of that treatment, for the most part, was rarely anti-Semitism. It was ignorance.

My 2013 visit to Van Buren taught me that I also needed more education about Christianity. I didn't know some things that devout Christians considered basic. Before a scheduled appointment at the high school, I walked around the village of Van Buren. The town looked like a place frozen in time with a one-room brick post office on a corner of Main Street. The old convenience store where I used to buy snacks after school was shuttered. From atop street lamp poles, black-and-orange banners in the Van Buren school colors fluttered in a breeze. I walked into the Van Buren United Methodist Church, the same brick church that had dominated the center of the village decades ago. I had hoped to speak to the pastor about the role of religion today in Van Buren schools. The pastor wasn't there, but the smell of apples, cinnamon, and sugar drew me to the basement; half a dozen women were assembling thirty-five apple pies for a church fund-raiser. One of the women, who had a child in the school system, said she helped out once a week with the afterschool Bible club at Van Buren Elementary School. The club would meet that very afternoon and sing praise songs, she told me. I had no idea what she meant, so she started singing one for me.

"Praise" refers to praising Jesus or God. I asked if I could visit the club. She said sure.

Van Buren had kicked Powell's program out of its classrooms but had let the afterschool club in many years later, in 2010. A Methodist church in Findlay rents the space from the school and seeks participants by sending an information sheet home to parents via children's teachers, the elementary school principal told me rather blithely. The afterschool group and how it disseminates information had never been an issue, said the principal, who had taught at Van Buren Elementary for more than a decade before taking the school's top job. Volunteers teach roughly fifty students, a little more than 10 percent of the elementary school's enrollment. As the program began that afternoon, the bearded pastor from Van Buren's Methodist church strummed a guitar and nudged the children sitting on the cafeteria floor to sing "This Little Light of Mine." Soon they were standing up, moving to the music, and clapping. The pastor sang another song about Jesus. That is a praise song, whispered the parent I had met at the church. The pastor ended his part by leading the children in prayer. "Help them so when we leave this place we can do it in Jesus's name," he said, his eyes closed as he prayed.

The children split into smaller groups for Bible study with different teachers, including a woman who was a retired Findlay public schools elementary teacher. She sat at a bench at one of the cafeteria tables and taught about twenty children sitting on a baseball blanket. The children learned different names for Jesus then moved over to sit at tables. Their task was to fill in the blanks on paper swords the teacher called swords of spirit. "When I am tempted to _____, God's word will help me defeat Satan," each paper said. Like Powell, the teacher in the afterschool program was not sure whether she liked the idea of schools teaching about the world's religions as an academic subject.[15]

The program, like the one in Findlay schools in the early 1980s, was held right after the school day ended. But it was on firmer legal ground. The ruling in the Findlay case no longer held. In 2001 the

Supreme Court ruled in favor of the Good News Club, an evange-
listic Christian program for children ages six to twelve. The program
wanted to use the Milford Central School facilities in upstate New
York to teach children Christian values immediately after school.
The school system, which didn't think it appropriate for its younger
students to have to walk by the club on their way out of school,
had barred the club from meeting in its facilities. Milford saw allowing the club as a violation of the separation of church and state,
especially since the club's aim was to convert unsaved children to
Christianity. But the Supreme Court, in a 6–3 decision, noted that
parents had to give permission for their children to attend and that
there was no evidence that young children could loiter nearby after
school ended. By keeping the Good News Club out, Justice Clarence Thomas wrote in the majority opinion, Milford was discrimi-
nating against the club because of its religious viewpoint. Religious
groups deserved the same access to school buildings as other organizations, the court ruled.[16] To me, the court's embrace of religious
programs on public school grounds was a step backward.

When I walked from Van Buren's elementary school to the
larger red-brick building next door, which houses grades 7 through
12, I found signs of hope and change. Some aspects, though, remained the same. A youth pastor sat in the main office when I got
there. During the lunch hour, he talked to students about Christian
youth club events, and once a week he served as the adult monitor
for the freshman/sophomore chapter of God's Knights, a Christian
club. The name stems from the school's mascot, the Black Knight,
and the club was founded in 2008 in memory of a girl who had died
of cancer during her junior year. The club, divided into different
groups by grade level, initially met in the cafeteria but later moved
into classrooms because of the noise level. As a result, the school
system had to provide adult monitors for the weekly meetings. The
youth pastor, a few teachers, and a teacher's aide acted as monitors.

The principal, Michael Brand, was a sign of the changes in my
former school system. He was very willing to talk about how the

school handled religion and how it worked to follow the law. Yes, Van Buren still allowed youth pastors, but Brand, who became principal in 1991, set rules for the visits. Pastors could not visit the lunchroom unless they had students there already involved in their clubs. The school no longer allowed religious assemblies nor had it allowed prayers at graduation during his tenure. He said my alma mater was a different world now because administrators during my time did not get the training he received in college about the separation of church and state. Like it or not, he said, he and his fellow administrators at Van Buren did not impose their beliefs on others, and neither did the teachers.[17]

Brand put off making a decision about allowing the God's Knights club for a year because he wanted to make sure the club was legal and that it did not pressure students to join. He made it clear to club members that the organization was not a school-sponsored activity. He has rejected the club's requests to hang up posters about God's Knights and its events. The middle and high school chapters have to find new members through word of mouth. But now that the club was a school staple, the principal had become a supporter because he believed the students had helped the school at large. The club's members supported one another and also supported members of the general school community. They talked about service. They talked about how to be good people. He visited the high school clubs about once a month and sometimes shared scripture and tied it back to the idea of making good choices at school.

I asked if he worried about the club cutting it too close to the line separating church and state, especially when he stood there and read scripture. He did it, he said, because the students asked. I didn't press him, but it seemed that he needed to keep more of a distance. The courts have always been clear that educators should play a hands-off role when it comes to promoting a particular religion. In 1984, Congress passed the Equal Access Act to clarify that high school students could form religious clubs if their school allowed other noncurriculum-related groups. The act emphasized that the meetings had to be both student-initiated and student-led and that teachers could act as monitors only in a nonparticipatory way.[18]

Students took the lead role in the two club meetings I saw, though the adults present did not just sit there quietly. At the first meeting, Rosemary Salisbury, a teacher's aide, spoke first to the thirteen juniors and seniors in attendance. She reminded them to always have Bibles and held one up. She also told them about adults in school who wanted their religious support. One teacher wanted club members to make sure he read the Bible daily, a promise he had made to himself. "Mr. Brand, be accountable to him," Salisbury said of the principal. "He asked for your prayers." She passed around slips of paper for students to write down their prayer requests and place into an Elmo Halloween treat bucket. She would take the bucket home and say the prayers. Her business done, she turned over the meeting to a seventeen-year-old senior, the designated group leader that day. "The biggest question we ask ourselves is, Why can't we hear God's voice?" he told his peers as they ate their lunches at desks in an American history and government classroom. He'd brought a video about that question, and they spent most of the half-hour meeting watching a motivational Christian speaker. After the video ended the teen meeting leader stood up and faced the group members, who bowed their heads to pray: "Thank you, Lord, for bringing us together. Thank you for bringing Linda here. Please allow her to be safe on the way back. In your name, we pray." Unlike during childhood, I was in that room voluntarily. I heard the student's prayer and viewed it in the way it was delivered, as something beautiful and heartfelt.

The students in God's Knights, just as the principal described, came off as spiritual and just plain nice. The group, several students said, gave them a needed break from the hectic pace of high school. Sometimes they watched videos together. Sometimes they talked about Bible verses and how they related to their own lives. They shared a common bond, a desire to have their faith take a large role in their lives. One girl, a seventeen-year-old junior, liked how talking about God with her classmates gave her week a recharge. She could sit in the classroom and not have to think about schoolwork or the drama that often went on among teens outside in the halls. She just thought about God. Then, afterward, she and her fellow club members took the light they felt in the room and spread it through the school. "It's so much better than if Jesus weren't in the school," she said.[19] I wondered whether all of her peers had the same sentiment. Some, I had already learned, considered themselves atheist. They, as well as less-devout Christians, may have had no interest in experiencing Jesus at school.

Members of God's Knights prayed at the school flagpole during the annual See You at the Pole prayer rally. They also went Christmas caroling with teachers and had conducted a prayer walk through the school after classes ended for the day. The school board gave permission for the prayer walk after hours, said Salisbury, who organized it. Students, along with parents and pastors, walked through the school and prayed over the rooms until every part of the school was covered in prayer. Salisbury treasured God's Knights as much as its members did. She said the students had often pulled her through a rough day. On Tuesday nights she ran an extension of the club at her home, leading the students in further discussions about religion. That spring of 2013 they were discussing a book they had read as a group, *Crazy Love: Overwhelmed by a Relentless God*, by Francis Chan, an evangelical Christian preacher. It was a little déjà vu of my conversations with the Lumberton, Texas, superintendent when Salisbury talked about Van Buren's unique situation as such a Christian-based community. The school board members, she told me, praised Jesus before their meetings began.[20]

Hope, then deflation. There was hope that Van Buren no longer allowed religious assemblies. There was disappointment that the principal thought it was okay to read scripture to a student Bible club and that a teacher's aide collected student prayer requests. There was disappointment, too, that a youth pastor still frequented the lunchroom. There was hope, though, that Van Buren was paying more attention to the world's religions in its middle and high school. The middle and high school principals pegged the change to sometime in the 1990s, perhaps partly prompted by amended state standards. In 2002, the Ohio Department of Education pushed the requirement to study Ohio history from seventh grade to the fourth grade. In sixth and seventh grade, Van Buren students learn about the world's religions as part of world history classes. By the time they finished both grades, they had learned basic information about Judaism, Christianity, Hinduism, Islam, and Buddhism.[21] A high school world history teacher said he included instruction about the world's religions where it fit in his course. Van Buren's educators saw world history classes as an imperative, especially since the school was in an isolated pocket of the country. They wanted the children to get an understanding of other religions and learn what Jews believed, what Hindus believed, what Muslims believed.

It gave me hope that a pair of teens I interviewed could be equally enthusiastic about God's Knights and learning about other faiths.[22] They agreed to an impromptu quiz, a shorter version of a religious literacy test author Stephen Prothero once gave his students at Boston University. They knew that the Koran was the holy book of Islam and that Jesus was born in Bethlehem. They could name the first five books of the Hebrew Bible, or Old Testament. They could define the Golden Rule. They, a boy and a girl, stumbled over Ramadan and what it was. "Is that Jewish?" the girl asked, giggling a little. "Or is it Muslim?" Still, they fared well, given that Prothero reported that most of his students flunked his quiz.[23] The girl said she liked learning about other faiths even as it reaffirmed why she believed that only Christ rose from the dead.

The middle school's history teachers perhaps gave me the most hope of all. Each talked of trying to go beyond what was in the textbook about the world's religions. The sixth-grade teacher covered the beginnings of Judaism and a little of Islam, Buddhism, Hinduism, and Confucianism as the students studied ancient civilizations. The seventh-grade teacher went deeper into Islam, covering the origins and the spread of the religion. He also regularly took the students on a tour of the mosque in Toledo, where a mosque member gave them a lecture about some of the basics of Islam. On one of those visits, the tour guide demonstrated how Muslims prayed for the students. Van Buren, so much more conservative than Wellesley, had never gotten backlash from parents about the field trips. So far only one family had refused to sign the permission slip for the mosque tour. Jack Marshall, who teaches those students, also worked hard to dispel stereotypes of Muslims.[24] He noted that every religion had people who went astray. He used the Ku Klux Klan as an example, talking about how the racist organization's members terrorized blacks and other minority groups in America from the 1920s to the 1960s in the name of Christianity. He tried to nudge students out of their comfort zone. "Nobody says all Christians are bad because stupid people wear white hats and burn crosses in someone's yard, so we shouldn't do that with other religions," he told them.

Has Van Buren moved forward since my time? Teachers were making an effort at least to expose their students to other religions. They had no blueprint to follow and their audience was not always receptive. Many of their students were taught from an early age that their religion was the only right one. Some students resisted the notion that not everyone thought the way they did. For others, the lessons about the world's religions turned into an "aha" moment because they simply had never thought about what others might believe. The toughest challenge was to counteract the prominent communal message that Christianity was the only religion to care about. The only houses of worship for miles around had crosses and an insurance company broadcast the solution to all problems with words painted on a cross on an outside wall: "Christ is the Answer."

Van Buren was not that unusual for Ohio, which in many ways seemed as much a part of the Bible Belt as the South did. As I visited Van Buren in 2013, a movement was afoot in the state legislature to give public high school students credit for religious courses they took off campus during regular school hours from private educators. The bill would treat the courses, of the same ilk as the classes Powell taught, as electives. By June 2014 the measure had passed into law. Under the new law, no public money can be spent on the classes and school districts can set standards for teacher qualifications.[25] Ohio's law followed the lead of South Carolina. What academic purpose does it serve to give credit for a class meant to make sure children stay devoted to the religion of their birth? Wouldn't it be better if states focused instead on approving measures that required students to take a class on comparative religions? I mentioned the notion of a required high school world religions class to Van Buren's principal before parting. He didn't pooh-pooh the idea. But he didn't see it as a reality in the near future. He would need more money in the budget to pay for a teacher for the course. He would need a teacher, too, who could teach a semester's class about different religions. In Van Buren, such an idea seemed out of reach. But it did not have to be.

CHAPTER SIX

Carefully Taught

ALYSSA DAVIS could not take her eyes off the objects lining the sill of the classroom window in her high school in Modesto, California. There was a cross, a menorah, a miniature Buddha, and a nearly six-inch-tall gold Buddha glinting from the sun. She didn't recognize the other objects but knew they were idols. The fourteen-year-old was terrified. She was apostolic, a Pentecostal Christian taught to shun religious idols. She sat at her desk in the world religions course and felt as if her body was growing heavier. She feared she would burn in hell if she stayed in this classroom. As teacher Sherry Mc-Intyre gave the first lectures of the semester, Alyssa prayed silently, "Heavenly God, don't let me go to hell for this." In her church, she learned that the Pentecostal way was the right way and to fear all other religions. But it was her freshman year at Johansen High. She wanted to get straight A's.[1]

Alyssa was a guinea pig in a Modesto city schools experiment that would eventually become touted as a national model for teaching about the world's religions. The year Alyssa started high school, in 2000, Modesto for the first time required all freshmen to take a half-semester course on the world's religions. It was a new graduation requirement and an unheard of approach elsewhere. Modesto, a city of roughly two hundred thousand, created the course after a dispute with religious leaders over whether it was appropriate to train teachers on gay rights. Modesto is just ninety miles east of San Francisco but far apart from the City by the Bay in its sensibilities. Numerous evangelical churches, some with congregations numbering in the thousands, call Modesto home, and the area is nicknamed California's Bible Belt. Before the freshman course was created, Modesto high schools wrapped instruction about religion into world history or world geography classes, and students in sixth or seventh grade received a smattering of instruction on world religions. If high schools had a course on world religions, it was an elective. Modesto educators wanted to require a survey course on religions for freshmen to fill a gap. Students who entered world history classes were woefully ignorant about the basics of the world's religions.[2]

While Wellesley thought sixth grade was the perfect time for a course on religion because it might prevent bullying, Modesto teachers preferred moving most instruction about religion to ninth grade, when they believed students were more mature and more ready for the material. Students would take a half semester of geography followed by a half semester about the world's religions. Teachers believed the religions part of the course could set the tone for each high school and instill respect for religious and other differences among students.

Modesto teachers also acted as if the course were a piece of glass that would break at the slightest touch. They set a slew of guidelines, influenced by advice from the First Amendment Center, in hopes that their schools would avoid fights with the community over the course. There would be no field trips to houses of worship, no guest speakers, and no role-playing related to religion, including trying on religious garments. Playing it fair with each religion was also central. The teachers chose *The Usborne Encyclopedia of World Religions* as their textbook because it devoted the same number of pages to each religion. At a minimum, teachers were asked to cover six religions in the nine-week course: Judaism, Christianity, Islam, Hinduism, Sikhism, and Buddhism. In other religion courses around the country, Sikhism was rarely included. Modesto teachers wanted to include the religion because of the large presence of Sikhs in their community. The course designers also gave teachers the option to add four other religions: Shintoism, Jainism, Taoism, and Confucianism. None of the issues that snared Tampa, Lumberton, and Wellesley in controversy happened here. Modesto instead grabbed the kind of news coverage that school systems adore—television features on CBS News and CNN and articles in local and national newspapers. I traveled to Modesto in the fall of 2013, thirteen years after the course started, to see if it lived up to its reputation as a national model. How well was the course reaching students? Was ninth grade really a better time to teach about the world's religions than sixth? Were the rules, created to avoid controversy, also a barrier?

Alyssa went home that first day of class and cried as she told her mother that she just could not stay in the course. Her mother told her to take the class and pray through it. Even as Alyssa prayed, she forced herself to listen to McIntyre, who had no idea that the teen, one of nearly forty students, was so apprehensive. Alyssa took the thin paperback textbook home and began reading the chapters about different religions and, to her surprise, found nothing that said "kill people" in regard to non-Christian religions and nothing that supported her church's contention that other religions worshipped the devil. Her teacher also helped her start to feel at ease. McIntyre did not belong to a particular religion and in fact embraced them all as different paths to the same goal. She helped Alyssa realize that those objects on the windowsill were just an introduction to an array of religions. Over the course's nine weeks, the teen learned more about the figures next to the Buddha statues. There was a statue of Confucius; a white ceramic statute of Guanyin, who stood for compassion in Buddhism; a figure representing Shiva, the Hindu god dancing in a circle of flames; and a miniature sculpture of Om, the sacred symbol for the sound of life in Hinduism. The young woman's almost paralyzing fear soon faded.

When they created the course, Modesto teachers hoped they could break through to the most skeptical and fearful students, particularly those from devout Christian families. They presumed these students and their parents might be a tough sell given the tenor of the times when the school system created the course. The school district in the late 1990s got into a tug-of-war over values with the city's evangelical Christian community. The superintendent at the time, James Enochs, was intent on training teachers and staff to be sensitive to gay rights issues after hearing about harassment of a gay boy in a Modesto high school. Other boys threw the boy in a shower, tore his gym clothes off him, and pushed his head into the toilet. Enochs listened as the boy's parents told him the story in his office and he felt ashamed. He had come from a generation that used to tell gay jokes without thinking, and he led a school district where such abuse could happen.

The superintendent set up a committee to design a tolerance policy and sent teachers and staff to workshops on sensitivity run by gay rights organizations. The then-pastor of Big Valley Church, one of the area's megachurches, accused the school system of advocating an alternative lifestyle. The school system, the pastor charged, was asking students to tolerate immoral behavior. Enochs received numerous letters from Big Valley congregants protesting the proposed policy, including one from a woman who told Enochs he was the devil incarnate for trying to push children into such a deviant lifestyle. The controversy only grew more volatile and weird. Incomprehensibly, at a board meeting, a man came in and put $2,000 in cash on a table. "This is the price you pay for leading our children down this path," he told the board, though he didn't explain what a few thousand dollars had to do with that accusation.[3] The school board supported the idea of a new policy against harassment of gays and others, but it was at loggerheads with the church community. Fearful that tensions would never ease, Enochs recruited the help of Charles Haynes, the senior scholar at the First Amendment Center, who had a reputation for mediating conflicts among schools and religious communities.

Haynes, soft-spoken with a slight southern drawl left over from his upbringing in Durham, North Carolina, has a master's from Harvard Divinity School and a doctorate in religious studies from Emory University. Since the 1980s, he had been a go-to person nationally on issues involving schools and the First Amendment. He was the last president of a group called the National Council on Religion in Public Education, which had pushed for more instruction about religion in schools until its efforts died in the mid-1980s. That group, like so many in the preceding decades, was a casualty of America's culture wars. It struggled to keep the focus on teaching about religion as an academic subject as Christians sought to bring back more religiosity and Christian values to the schools.

Researchers date the start of the movement to teach about religion in public schools to 1963, though there were attempts to promote the concept as early as the 1940s. The American Council on Education, which represents college presidents, issued three reports between 1944 and 1953 calling for the factual study of religion in public schools.[4] Those reports outlined the mixed-bag treatment of religion in schools at the time, including Bible readings and prayer but also scattered attempts to incorporate academic study of religion. The 1953 report said religion could and should be studied "in the same way as the economic and political institutions and principles of our country should be studied."[5] The report described schools that avoided teaching about religion because of fear of giving offense. But it also highlighted a school where students learned about eight religions in a sophomore-level world cultures course and also took field trips to museums, a synagogue, and a Catholic church, and attended panel discussions on religion. Such examples were rare, and the report's recommendations pushed for creating experimental projects in select communities to figure out the best grade to teach about religion and the best way to incorporate it into the study of history. It was a report ahead of its time, issued in the midst of bitter court battles over whether it was appropriate for schools to preach one particular religion to students.

Educators and religion scholars today generally agree that it was Supreme Court Justice Tom C. Clark's famous words in the 1963 school prayer ruling, *Abington v. Schempp*, that did the most to persuade religion scholars, educators, religious leaders, and politicians to work together to give religion a strong academic place in public schools. Clark responded to those who felt getting rid of the prayer and Bible readings would establish a "religion of secularism in the schools." He said schools could not oppose or show hostility to religion, then laid out what they could do: "It might well be said that one's education is not complete without a study of comparative religion or the history of religion and its relationship to the advancement of civilization."[6] Shortly afterward, California and Florida passed laws authorizing schools to teach secular courses in religion, while legal and education officials in at least seven other states advised schools that they could teach religion in an objective way.[7] In 1964, numerous players supported Clark's call to include the academic study of the Bible and world religions in the public schools. The American Association of School Administrators, which represented principals and other school administrators, issued a report calling for better preparation of teachers and more accurate, useful materials on religion.[8] At Wright State University in Dayton, Ohio, Nicholas Piediscalzi founded the university's Department of Religion and, in 1968, cowrote a handbook for teachers on handling religion appropriately and educationally. Professional and religious organizations also used the guide to promote the study of religion in schools.

For the next fifteen years after the 1963 ruling there was a flurry of activity, including the creation of curriculum materials, training and certification programs for teachers, and the founding of national, regional, and state organizations to support the efforts.[9] Justice Clark's words led to an awakening among teachers about the need to teach about religion, particularly within history, but the awakening was never widespread, said Piediscalzi, who at eighty-two has never lost his passion for advocating for more instruction about religion in schools.[10] In 1972, he cofounded the Public Education Religious Studies Center, and he and his colleagues trained two groups: English teachers who wanted to teach about the Bible and its place in literature, and social studies teachers who wanted to learn how to better incorporate religion in history classes. Around the same time, Florida State University ran curriculum projects related to religion, and in Newton, a Boston suburb, an English teacher was developing a reputation as a pioneer because he had created a course known as the Bible in Literature.

There were even state efforts promoting classes. Pennsylvania created two courses, Religious Literature of the West and Religious Literature of the East, and initially provided funding for the western literature course and teacher workshops. In 1973, Clark, the justice who wrote the *Schempp* decision, spoke at a symposium on religion and education to celebrate the prayer ruling's tenth anniversary and the opening of the Wright State center on academic study of religion in public schools. Clark tried to motivate teachers and professors to keep working to make religion a part of the curriculum even as they faced skepticism and reluctance from various corners. He commiserated with the educators: "Some days it's going to be hard sledding; some days you'll get disappointed . . ." But he told the group he believed they would succeed and create effective programs. Then they would know they had helped not only make their community but their state and the nation a better place to live morally and spiritually.[11]

By the 1980s, efforts were fading. In Pennsylvania, thousands of courses were introduced only to disappear when funding dried up.[12] The Wright State center persevered through the 1970s and into the start of the 1980s but stopped most of its activities by 1986. An economic recession hit Ohio, making it impossible to rely on funds from the state or to raise money from foundations. Also, the culture wars of the 1970s and 1980s affected the center's and others' work to promote teaching about religion in the schools. Evangelical Christians were renewing pushes for lessons on creationism. The fears of Alyssa Davis about the Modesto world religions class were a throwback to this period. The preaching of religion in schools, seemingly driven out by the 1963 ruling, was also making a comeback. What I experienced in Van Buren was common in little towns in rural areas. Piediscalzi and his colleagues had no luck getting buy-in for their training in many schools near them in southern Ohio. He had a farm in tiny Peebles and, every Friday, the schools would have religious instruction and rituals and singing of the hymns. The demise of the early movement saddened him. He had invested his professional life in it with great hope, only to watch his efforts fizzle.

National associations and Haynes worked to resurrect the movement. In 1984, the National Council for Social Studies approved guidelines on how to address religion in history curricula. It would revise those again more than a decade later.[13] Also in the mid- to late 1980s, several studies reported that religion was being downplayed or ignored in most textbooks.[14] Haynes became a vocal proponent of improving textbooks and promoted new ideas to give religion a bigger academic presence in schools. He lobbied for a two-pronged approach. First, teach about the First Amendment and what it means to give everyone religious freedom, and then move on to teaching about the world's religions. He also brought together educational and religious organizations to design guides for schools on how to teach about religion and still heed the First Amendment. He worked to make schools understand that it was okay to let a student pray and for religious groups to exist. It just wasn't okay for teachers and adults in the school to lead religious activities. Between 1988 and 2006 he was the prime mover who united groups to create nine statements of common ground on religion and public education.[15]

Teaching about religion would also get a boost when studying world religions became a part of most states' standards for social studies and geography by the late 1990s and early 2000s.[16]

It would take the 9/11 attacks to give the movement its biggest boost.[17] The attacks by Muslim terrorists highlighted Americans' ignorance about Islam and about religion in general and motivated educators and policymakers to pay more attention. "It is no longer a question of whether schools *should* teach children about Islam. They *must* teach them—about other religions as well. It is a responsibility, a duty," John Seigenthaler, the First Amendment Center's founder, wrote in the foreword to a 2007 guide about religion and schools.[18] In 2010, the American Academy of Religion, a group of religion scholars, tried to expand the movement more by producing a guide for teachers on religion as an academic subject. Diane Moore, a religion professor at Harvard Divinity School, chaired the group that created the guidelines, which included such tips as making careful selections of guest speakers or avoiding them altogether. Moore, like Piediscalzi, also had run a training program for teachers. Hers gave teachers a certificate in religious studies in education. But that program, which began in the 1970s, closed in 2010, a victim of funding cuts. A year later Moore began resurrecting some of the program in a different form, offering online training for teachers and workshops through the new Religious Literacy Project. There remains no concerted national effort even though few educators and policymakers disagree whether students should learn about the world's religions as a part of history. For now, individuals like Moore and Haynes, some foundations interested in interfaith dialogue among students, and a few school districts, such as Modesto and Wellesley, are leading a free-for-all movement.[19]

Initially, Modesto wanted Haynes for his skills as a mediator rather than for his background as a leader in religion and education issues. Expecting a small group, Haynes came to Modesto on a Saturday to meet a committee reviewing the tolerance policy. Instead, at least ninety people greeted him when he entered a high school cafeteria.[20] They sat in different clumps. The pastors were at the back. The teachers were in the front. Many people had their arms crossed, as if signaling they would not budge from their stance. Rather than confront the issue head-on, Haynes began with a history lesson as he walked in the front of the cafeteria speaking into a microphone. He knew both sides had spent the past six to eight months talking past each other. He wanted to find a way to move the conversation forward.

He reminded the group, he recounted to me over lunch at a Washington, DC, café, that they shared a common history and an agreement, the US Constitution, and that people of different religions and cultures are part of that agreement. The country was founded based on a set of principles and ideals, a vision that made each person in the room American.[21] He set a task of getting the group to commit to ground rules for how they would deal with each other. He reminded them of the First Amendment and of the rights it set, both to allow the free exercise of religion and to prevent laws that would promote a particular religion. The issue may have centered on gay rights, but at its core the controversy was about religion. Haynes met with the group all day and guided them into a discussion about the Three Rs Project he founded in the early 1990s with educators in California. The three R's stood for rights, responsibility, and respect, and the project, run in a few states, promotes literacy about the freedom of religion and the First Amendment. He talked to the group about the right to religious liberty and moved from rights ultimately to the idea of respect. "Can we all agree to debate our differences with civility?" he asked, emphasizing that civility was not tolerance. It was showing respect for the rights of others. It didn't mean that they had to think a particular religion was great or that they had to accept gay rights or homosexuality. Tension in the room began to dissipate. People started saying they could agree to that concept of respect. The school system officials agreed, saying they would not create a tolerance policy and instead would create a new Rights, Respects, and Responsibility policy that would also become part of a character program. Haynes never anticipated that a course on world religions would grow out of those discussions. He didn't think it was politically possible, given the divide between the evangelical Christian community and the school system.

Modesto was a city trying to cope with huge demographic shifts. Founded in 1870 at the crossing of the Tuolumne and San Joaquin rivers, Modesto drew its early population from nearby river towns because people wanted to live close to the new railroad. Early Modesto was the Wild West, which became abundantly clear on a visit to the McHenry Museum. A museum volunteer, Bill Bucknam, immediately offered to become my tour guide. He also turned out to be a retired Modesto teacher who was one of the first to teach the freshman religions course. Lanky and a tad goofy, Bucknam donned cowboy chaps and posed for a photo in front of an old stage coach as he described Modesto's origins as a den of iniquity. There was gambling, corruption, and gunfights. By the 1900s, Bucknam's ancestors had moved to the area and they helped build an irrigation system that laid the groundwork for flourishing agriculture in the middle of the desert. The Gallo winery established its headquarters in Modesto around 1930. The area's Hispanic population began to appear in the 1950s as large waves of migrants came to pick grapes and almonds. Blue Diamond Growers made the city its home base, and the sixty-six-year-old Bucknam, who was born in the area, recalled watching workers strike the trees with rubber mallets to knock the almonds down. Machines now do that job.

The most prominent church during Bucknam's childhood in the 1950s and 1960s was the First Baptist Church. By the 1960s and 1970s, several megachurches had been founded and the area became more of a Bible Belt as an influx of people moved there from Texas, Oklahoma, Arkansas, and Arizona. In 1970 Modesto, then a city of sixty-two thousand, was still overwhelmingly white.[22] But by 2000 it had more than tripled in size and become more diverse.

Just a little less than two-thirds of the population was white, while a quarter was Hispanic, and the rest came from a variety of ethnic and racial groups. By 2010 about half of the residents were white and Hispanics had become more than a third of the population. The next biggest groups were Asian or Asian Indian.[23] The area now has temples for Sikhs, Hindus, and Buddhists and a worship space for Muslims. Since its early years the city has had a Jewish population, albeit a small one.[24]

Bucknam gave me a tour of mostly old Modesto in the museum while Yvonne Taylor, also one of the course's founding teachers, gave me a modern-day tour in her Honda Civic.[25] She retired from Modesto schools in 2009 after thirty-eight years of teaching, and she and her husband, a retired police detective, hosted me in their home in one of Modesto's newer neighborhoods, where each house sits on a manicured lot with almost no yard. Taylor, who had been married for forty years and had two grown daughters, came to Modesto in 1971 when the city was still fairly homogenous. Self-deprecating, she described herself as a Valley Girl because she'd grown up in Lodi, thirty-five miles north of Modesto. She had a vivacious personality but Taylor's years as an educator defined her more than anything else. Her immaculate home was decked out for the fall, with candles and decorations in autumn's hues of orange, red, and brown. On the tour she gave me, she was in nonstop teacher mode. As she drove she pointed out fields of corn and groves of almond and persimmon trees. She stopped the car and we walked into an almond grove where thousands of almonds sprinkled the ground and crunched under our feet. The scenery switched from rural to more urban as we entered Modesto's tidy downtown dotted with flags that read "American Graffiti." Modesto inspired the film of the same name because teenagers cruised the main drag in the 1950s. Modesto now was a city of contrasts, with richer neighborhoods gated because of a high crime rate and a poorer section, where it was not uncommon to spot a homeless man sleeping on the steps of a church.

Taylor, known as Modesto's most vocal advocate for its religions course, was passionate in her effort to wipe out intolerance. She expressed disgust that, every May, Ku Klux Klan members gathered in the nearby town of Tracy to celebrate Hitler's birthday. It grated, too, to know that nearly every non-Christian faith had faced some kind of hate incident in Modesto before and after the religions course was created. The city's sole synagogue, which has had around five hundred members in recent years, was vandalized with anti-Semitic graffiti a few times over the past fifteen years. One of the more publicized incidents happened in 2009 when vandals used black spray paint to draw swastikas and write epithets and crossed out Jewish symbols on the temple's walls.[26] Taylor pointed out Shree Ram Mandir, a Hindu temple bordered by a white metal fence on the city's northern edge, by farm fields and the Gallo winery. On the outside the temple resembled a warehouse, but it was not nondescript enough to escape the acts of bigots. Someone once killed a calf and dumped it there in the aftermath of 9/11. Hindus consider cows sacred.[27] Taylor mused that the temple probably started raising an American flag daily to emphasize that its members were Americans too.

The Sikhs in Modesto and nearby towns have faced some of the toughest times, and I heard about some of their experiences when I visited the Sikh Temple of Modesto during my first full day in the city. The temple has 9,000 registered members.[28] Sikhs have been commonly mistaken for Muslims, harassed verbally, and sometimes beaten. Male Sikhs traditionally wear turbans to wrap their hair and females also wear head coverings that closely resemble the Muslim hijab. In September 2001, less than a week after the 9/11 attacks, a sixty-nine-year-old Sikh man was found dead in an irrigation canal in a town near Modesto. The man's family and the Sikh community have long believed the man was the victim of a hate crime. An autopsy found no signs of foul play, but even a decade later, area

Sikhs recalled that incident to me as an example of the problems they have faced.[29] The Modesto Sikh temple, referred to as a *gurdwara*, was founded in 1978 in a small white house, then moved into a larger temple in 1998. The most eye-catching building on the Modesto site was an all-white temple topped with three onion-shaped domes. "God is one" were the words inscribed in blue in Punjabi and English above a building called Langar Hall, where Sikhs eat a communal meal every Sunday. Above the words was a traditional Sikh symbol, which stands for *Ik Onkhar*, or "One God," the first two words in the Sikh holy book, known as the Guru Granth Sahib.

Gurbax Kaur Shergill, the principal of the temple's religious school, acted as my guide and teacher, as did some of the religious school students. Shergill, who teaches chemistry at a public high school in Merced, near Modesto, wore a pink flowered tunic on top of pink pants and a pink scarf, called a *dupatta*, around her hair. She, like most Sikhs, came from Punjab, a state in India. Out of respect to Sikh practices, I wore a scarf around my hair and took my shoes off as soon as I entered any of the buildings. Women and girls had their heads covered and, like Shergill, wore sari-like tunics and long pants in a rainbow of colors: pinks, purples, greens, oranges. The boys and men wore turbans. Sikhs, students told me, do not cut their hair because they consider it a gift from God. They wear particular clothing and items to meet the obligations of their faith, including a *kirpan*, a sword that is a symbol of dignity, power, and unconquerable spirit.[30] At Shergill's urging, I walked around the temple and entered the worship space. I was nervous about disturbing the service but the sight of men and women moving in and out of the gymnasium-sized room reassured me. Sitting on the carpeted floor on the women's side, I watched as an occasional worshipper went to the front of the worship space, clasped his or her hands, and bowed and knelt in front of the holy book set on a platform. An attendant waved a huge whisk that resembled a yellow feather over the book. Nearby two men played harmoniums while a third musician accompanied them on a set of tabla drums. Dressed in white, the men sang prayers in Punjabi.

I ran into Shergill as I was about to leave and she urged me to join her at the communal lunch. We stood in line with dozens of men, women, and children and accepted portions of various Punjabi dishes from volunteers staffing the buffet. There was warm Indian flatbread, yogurt, garbanzo beans, and a dish that looked like white porridge. Afterward, Shergill headed to a nearby sink to wash away, she said, the smell of curry that seeps into her hair, purse, and clothes. I washed as well, but the slightly sweet smell stuck with me as I drove away, a memory of my introduction to Sikhism. During lunch Shergill had told me she believed so many people misunderstood Sikhs because Sikhs had not worked hard to educate others about their religion. Too often the religious school at the temple had to coach parents how to deal with schools when their children faced taunts because of their head coverings. She had high hopes for Modesto's course on world religions and wished the high school she worked at required the same class.[31]

But having the class at the high school level did not prevent problems for the youngest Sikhs. Bhupinder Padda started kindergarten in Modesto schools wearing a *patka*, a miniturban, over his uncut hair. After one year, he stopped wearing it and demanded to have his hair cut because so many of his classmates made fun of him and he already felt like an outcast.[32] Though Bhupinder was born in the United States, his parents had spoken only Punjabi to him since birth. His father, an operations supervisor at the Gallo winery, and mother had come to the United States in 1990. Bhupinder could say only his name, his birthday, and a few other words in English when he started school. Worse, the boy who would grow to be six feet, four inches as an adult was the tallest child in his kindergarten class. As I met with Bhupinder and his parents one evening in their living room, his mother remembered how she cried over her son's pain and his decision not to wear the *patka*. She didn't want her son teased, but she also wanted him to stick to his faith's traditions. That his son no longer felt comfortable wearing the *patka* hurt Bhupinder's father but he understood. When Bhupinder's father came to the United States, he cut his hair that same year and stopped wearing a turban except at temple. There were fewer Sikhs in Modesto back then and he thought he might not get a job if he looked too different.

Bhupinder took the world religions course in 2005 at Johansen High School from Yvonne Taylor, who lives on the same street as his family. Did the course make a difference, I asked? He said yes and no. Yes, because he learned about other religions, but no, because he could hear snickering when the students watched a video about India and its religions. Friends sometimes were curious and asked him questions about Sikhism, but all Bhupinder wanted to do was avoid the situation. He didn't want to stand out as different and the course highlighted religious differences. His father, though, remembered something positive from the course. One day his son came home from school and announced, "Hey, Dad, at least now these kids know who I am."

Now twenty-two, Bhupinder majored in biochemistry at the University of the Pacific. After college graduation he began work as an operations manager at Frito-Lay. He thinks the high school course made the biggest difference for him in college. He felt more at ease talking about religion, whether his own or someone else's, in college and credited his high school with giving him that confidence. It surprised him to see that many of his college peers had almost no background on the world's religions. Many didn't even know Sikhism was a religion. The biggest problems for his family have been in the community at large. Even now, when Bhupinder's family stops at a red light on the way to a Sikh event or service, strangers sometimes flip a middle finger at his father, who wears his turban to religious events. Bhupinder keeps his dark hair short and still will not wear a turban.

—⚇—

In Modesto schools, the world's religion course has been an attempt to counteract such ignorance by planting the seed in children's minds that the right approach is to respect differences rather than make fun of them. The group of Modesto history teachers did not work in isolation. The teachers designed the course, then shared a rough draft with religious leaders and listened to concerns, including a complaint from a rabbi that the course was too basic and treated religion too gently. He didn't like that the course did not cover the Holocaust. The teachers responded by saying they did cover the Holocaust in sophomore-level world history classes. They eventually won over most religious leaders as they emphasized that the course's intent was to cover the development of each religion and its basic traits rather than major historical or current events.[33]

The teachers' biggest priority, in the aftermath of the clash with evangelical Christian leaders over gay rights training, was avoiding controversy. They ruled out field trips because they knew that some parents would not allow their children to enter another house of worship. They were worried, too, that they could not control what religious leaders of other institutions might say to the students. The teachers would serve as the academic experts for the course, and no one else, including guest speakers or clergy, would step into that role. The teachers worked with First Amendment Center staff to develop guidelines for anyone teaching the course. Their list came mostly from guides created over the years by First Amendment experts and religious scholars.[34] The guidelines were explicit about how teachers should handle themselves. In other school systems I visited, teachers were unsure if it was okay to talk openly about their faith so they made their own decision about it. Modesto teachers were instructed to teach the course and run their classroom without showing any advocacy for a religious or nonreligious point of view. They were told that their role was neither expert nor advocate and that they should encourage open inquiry without judgment. They were urged not to ask students to reveal their religious beliefs and one of the most detailed rules dealt with a teacher's own faith.

Modesto's guidelines said that when students asked a teacher about his or her own religious beliefs, the teacher should either decline to answer, stating that it would be inappropriate to include personal beliefs in class discussions, or the teacher could reveal his or her faith with a caveat. The teacher must say it was his or her own personal belief and then reinforce the role of objectivity in the classroom. The guidelines even told teachers not to use documentary videos unless the district's world geography/religions curriculum committee had approved them. The founding teachers wanted to leave little room for missteps. They also wanted to start teaching the classes with as much knowledge as possible.

The first teachers of the world religions course went through extensive training. They listened to instruction about the First Amendment from the First Amendment Center's staff, and many teachers soon viewed themselves as more than educators about the world's religions. They were also advocates for and enforcers of the First Amendment in their own schools. Taylor and the school system's curriculum coordinator, Jennie Sweeney, both worked at Johansen High and ran into conflicts with front office staff, who kept putting "Merry Christmas" on the marquee outside the school. Sweeney took on the battle first. The school at first responded by posting a tiny "Happy Hanukkah" sign in the office and leaving "Merry Christmas" on the marquee. Taylor took on the cause the next year and showed the school administrator what his own handbook said, that educators cannot give preference to one faith over another in a public setting.

Taylor, a Methodist, taught religious school at her church every Sunday, but as a teacher she kept that out of the classroom. She believed that her colleagues could teach world religions in a calm, neutral voice, and that schools could support that by keeping religious celebrations off school grounds. As part of the training, during the few years of the course the teachers also visited several different houses of worship, including the Sikh temple, the city's Muslim worship space, a Greek Orthodox church, Hindu and Buddhist temples, and a synagogue. Before the course began, religion scholars from nearby universities lectured teachers on Buddhism, Islam, and Christianity. But after those first years of heavy training, funds became limited. As teachers retired or quit teaching the course, new ones were not offered the same in-depth training. They were instead given an option of proving they had taken a course in world religions at the college level or of watching thirty hours of videos of college lectures on religion. They were also asked to read a book on the world's religions. Sweeney acted as watchdog for that training until 2007, when her curriculum coordinator position was eliminated to save money.

When I visited Modesto in 2013, a new coordinator had just been appointed and training was returning after a five-year absence. The course itself had changed little, though school district administrators say they would like to make the course higher-level to match national standards for freshman work. For years, teachers had relied on a prescribed curriculum kept in binders and on many of the original handouts and videos. The biggest constant was the same textbook with photos that showed Jewish and Muslim worshippers in the most religious garb. Judaism in the textbook was described as having two types of adherents, Orthodox or non-Orthodox, while, in fact, the religion has many more branches. Some of the covers of the textbooks, which were reused each year, had begun to fall off. The teachers, while they did not ignore current events, said they focused on teaching the history of religion more than contemporary religion. They knew they could not cover every aspect in a nine-week course. Maybe if they had a year, they could go deeper. Each classroom, as part of a districtwide policy, also paid homage to nine character traits—courage, honesty, loyalty, respect, responsibility, civility, compassion, initiative, and perseverance—that represented core community values, another outgrowth of the clash over gay rights.

But no two classrooms could look exactly the same, given the different personalities of teachers. I spent the most time with

McIntyre, who had taught Alyssa Davis that first year of the course. McIntyre teaches about ten religions during the course, and every nook and cranny of the classroom showed her passion for inclusiveness and respect of all religions. She lamented that she lacked a Sikh symbol to join the array of objects on the windowsill that overlooked a garden below on the grounds of Johansen High. Above her whiteboard at the front was the popular "Coexist" bumper sticker, which uses religious symbols for each letter. There was a "Teach Peace" banner and yet another larger banner with the symbols of eighteen different religions. A small placard quoted Gandhi: "We must become the change we want to see in the world." Her classroom was a spillover of what the fifty-year-old mother of six had in her home. She stored a collection of religious objects in a curio cabinet, including small and large Buddha figures, a menorah, a cross, and models of Hindu gods. On a living room bookshelf she had a copy of the New Testament in Hawaiian; a Koran in Arabic; a second Koran in English; and a Bible that belonged to her grandparents. One of her favorite books compares the sayings of Jesus and Buddha. "You live and breathe this," I said to McIntyre when she gave me the religion tour in her home. "Yes," she nodded with a smile. She was a true religion junkie.

McIntyre taught the same class five times a day to roughly forty students at a time. Most were freshmen, though some were upperclassmen who'd either flunked the course previously or didn't take it in ninth grade for some reason. "R-E-S-P-E-C-T," Aretha Franklin sang from McIntyre's computer stereo as students walked into their first world religions class of the unit in the fall of 2013. I sat toward the back as McIntyre used most of the first class to set ground rules for discussion. She used a handout called "Listening with Care," distributed by the Anti-Defamation League in 1998. She instructed students to write out the acronym ICARE and fill in the blanks by each letter. "I" stood for identifying the purpose of the communication, such as were they listening for information? "C" stood for concentrating on what the speaker was saying. "A" meant they should attend to the speaker, tune out distractions. "R" referred to reflecting on how the speaker felt as he or she talked, and "E" stood for encouraging the speaker to keep talking if you were not sure you understood what had been said. She coached students how to ask questions in a class where it's easy to offend. "The wrong way to ask a question is, 'Well, that's really stupid, why do people believe that?' A better way to word it would be, 'Wow, that's really interesting,'" said McIntyre, whose flowery skirt swung against her legs as she walked back and forth in front of the classroom. She emphasized the delicacy of the subject matter. "This is a world religions class," she said. "There are wars fought over this stuff." I saw her at home and at school. Around her own children and around forty teens at a time at school, McIntyre seemed like she had limitless energy. I knew, from talking with her, that she was indeed human and was tired after work. But in front of the classroom she had a knack for connecting with youth. Part of it could have been her word choice. No other teacher I knew referred to religions as "this stuff."

She described herself and Taylor, two of the four original teachers of the course, as akin to soldiers in their defense of the class. From the start, they worried that the community might balk. They worried about negative press. Instead, they developed something that brought them mostly kudos, a fact McIntyre was not shy about sharing with her students. She showed them a 2008 clip from the *CBS Evening News* of Taylor teaching the world religions class. The story was called "Teaching, not Preaching in the Bible Belt." The students seemed to be in various stages of interest. When McIntyre asked them to draw a line under ICARE in the lesson about being good listeners, one teen mumbled, "I don't." This class mixed in students of all levels in a school with tensions related more to race and ethnicity than religion. Johansen, one of the city's seven public high schools, had about 1,700 students. Most were Hispanic, a quarter were white, and the rest came from various other ethnic and racial groups.[35] The principal, who was new in the fall of 2013, and his assistants stood in several areas during lunch keeping watch because of competing Hispanic gangs. Students cannot wear two pieces of clothing that are red and blue because those are gang colors. McIntyre, always worried about the course's future, has approached each new principal at the school to gauge support for the class. The principal I met in 2013 was not that familiar with the class but supported the concept. As he juggled lunch duty, he told me that he wanted the school's students to know what was out there in the world, whether they leave Modesto or not; only 35 percent will go to college.

McIntyre, knowing that some students may never get it because they simply do not care, nevertheless always tries to emphasize the course's importance. She and other teachers saw a need in the community and created the course, she told her students. As the news clip from 2008 ended, she promised them that they would remember this class long after they graduated. "This," McIntyre said, looking out at the rows and rows of students, "is stuff you're going to encounter every day, different religions." She took the students through the same PowerPoint presentation she has used for years, beginning with an explanation of the First Amendment, the religious freedom clause, and the line that separates church from state. She lectured in a chipper style. She connected the language of the Constitution to life today. "You cannot, no matter what your religion tells you, you cannot come to school naked," she said, prompting laughter from the teens. "If your religion says you need to be naked all of the time, I'm sorry."

The next day she showed the class a video about the Constitution and freedom of religion in schools. The video included a clip about Jessica Ahlquist, who had protested a prayer plaque hanging in her Cranston, Rhode Island, high school auditorium just a few years before. Jessica, an atheist, wanted her school to follow the rules and not promote religion. She sued her school and won but not without duress. She faced threats and name-calling, and police had to escort her at her school.[36] "No matter what you feel, imagine being the only girl speaking up," McIntyre said before launching into a PowerPoint presentation about the teacher's hero, Roger Williams. The seventeenth-century theologian became known as a champion of religious freedom when he left Massachusetts for Rhode Island to form a colony for religious minorities who felt their rights were trampled on in the Bay State.

That same day, a student came up to McIntyre in tears. A senior, she did not believe in any religion and said she did not want to learn about religions. McIntyre tried levity in response, saying she felt the same way about math. The girl had come to class late and missed the video that partly featured an atheist teen. In more than a decade, very few students had protested about the class. The school system has developed an opt-out policy that required parents to meet with school administrators and discuss why they didn't want their child to take the course. The student then would get an alternate curriculum, one that was all geography. McIntyre, faced with the fearful senior, wanted to do everything she could to keep the student. She tried to reassure her that the class was not attempting to change her beliefs and she gave the student her stump talk for the course.[37] "I'm telling you, 'I'm not here to preach. I'm not here to convince you religion is the way to go.' You're going to meet religious people out there in the world, and the more you know about them, the more you know how to handle the situation, the more you understand them, the easier it will be."

She implored the student to return the next day and give her a chance. "Please," she said. "Okay," the student replied. The next day, the student came to class.

"'Teach, not preach,' that's our motto," McIntyre said at the beginning of her lecture the following day. She began a new PowerPoint presentation, and the first slide was of the oft-cited quote by Supreme Court Justice Tom C. Clark in the 1963 ruling that kicked prayer out of the schools. A person's education was not complete without a study of comparative religions, Clark wrote. Educators,

McIntyre told her students, could not teach world history without teaching about religion. It would be just wrong to ignore religion. She showed a slide of a tiny passage from the Williamsburg Charter, a 1988 document created by representatives of American's main faiths, particularly Protestant, Catholic, and Jewish, as well as secularists, and by political leaders and scholars. It was presented at a ceremony in Williamsburg, Virginia, because that city played a role as the cradle of religious liberty in America. McIntyre gave students a moment to read the words she had excerpted: "Religious liberty, freedom of conscience, is a precious, fundamental and inalienable right. A society is only as just and free as it is respectful of this right for its smallest minorities and least popular communities."[38] She saw that slide as one of the most important ones in the class. Respect. She wanted students to soak in the message she had sprinkled in at the start of the course with Aretha Franklin's famous song. "A right for one is a right for another. You can't just let another person be abused. We have to stand up for each other," she said to teens mostly wearing jeans, T-shirts, and flip-flops.

She also explained the purpose of religion and how people used it today to answer questions that may seem unanswerable, such as "Why do we die?" She taught the definitions of agnostic and atheist, terms also covered in a section of the textbook. McIntyre viewed the material as more seventh-grade level than high school level. But she worried more about teaching students to respect other religions than teaching them the intricacies of different faiths. She gave a multiple-choice exam and did not encourage discussion. Nor did she invite students to speak about their religions in class. I questioned the wisdom of that, and she responded that she wanted to avoid having a discussion that might go awry.

The founding teachers made a choice to keep the course simple and to avoid doing anything that could be taken the wrong way. They wanted success. When the attacks of 9/11 occurred, a year after the course began, the teachers were petrified about how it would play out in their classrooms. Anger, misunderstandings, and misinformation about Islam were spreading everywhere. The plan had been to not cover Islam until after the winter break. The teachers decided to stay on course. By the time they discussed Islam in class, feelings were not as raw. Teachers stuck to the script they had for Islam, teaching the nuts and bolts of the religion, about Mohammed and his background, about the daily life of an observant Muslim, and about jihad. McIntyre defined jihad the same way in 2001 after the 9/11 attacks and in 2013 after the Boston Marathon bombings. She talked about how jihad was an internal struggle for Muslims, a war within you to be a good person, to live a good life, to show the world what it means to be a good Muslim. She did not entirely ignore the dark side of religion. She again told her students in plain talk the message she wanted them to hear: terrorists are awful people, so it shouldn't be a surprise that they drag their religion down with them. But there are people from other religions who have done horrible things in the name of religion, too. "It's people who screw things up, not the religion," she said.[39]

No controversy has ever arisen out of the course, and it has met one of its basic goals, McIntyre and her colleagues said: students enter world history classes better prepared. Teachers no longer have to backtrack and explain the religious background of Gandhi, for example. Students at least know what it means when someone says "nirvana" or "karma," or refers to a Sikh turban. McIntyre believes the course makes a difference based on anecdotal accounts. About three years ago she was buying mattresses and a former student was working at the store. He immediately wanted to tell the teacher how her class had made a difference for him. He recalled how he was at a family gathering and someone made a stereotypical comment about Hindus. So he stood up and told that person he was wrong. McIntyre had encouraged him and his classmates to always stand up for the rights of the smallest groups. And the young man remembered that.

So did Alyssa Davis. She started speaking up when peers made fun of a few girls who wore hijabs because they were Muslim. She admonished her peers: "Hey, it's not cool." Now, as a twenty-seven-year-old, when she saw someone in a hijab or turban or sari, she looked at them differently than in the past. She may smile at them a little wider to let them know that in her view they're okay. She knew religious minorities faced so much, not just in Modesto but everywhere. The class also made her question her own religion and made her angry at her church, which had worked to turn her against other faiths. When she learned that Allah was just the Arabic name for God and not something evil, she was furious at her church. By the time the class was over she wished it had lasted a full year. That scared girl the first day of class ended up appreciating everything she had learned about religion, she told me as we chatted in a Starbucks in a Modesto shopping plaza.

The girl who once wore only long skirts to school showed up for the interview in a peach-colored shirt and black pants. She now worked full-time as a telephone operator for the Stanislaus Medical Society and was taking classes at Modesto Junior College. She identified herself as a nondenominational Christian and had abandoned the Pentecostal church years ago. Her dream was to run a day-care center and she planned to make sure she understood the children's different faiths so they were comfortable in the classroom.

Chapter Seven

Raising Religiously
Literate Americans

MODESTO HAD HOPED to serve as a model that other school systems would replicate. That has not happened. It took until 2014 for
the course to gain notice in its own state. That August, state lawmakers passed a resolution recommending that all school systems in California consider adopting Modesto's world religions course. There
was no force behind that resolution, though it was a symbolic moment for McIntyre and Taylor, who had fought so hard to keep the
course and promote its merits. Sadly, there has never been a nationwide movement to make the world's religions a more integral part
of education, despite the attempts of Haynes and so many others.
Modesto's course, as well as some of what I saw in other parts of the
country, could teach numerous lessons to school districts. Modesto's
course is required for every high school freshman. It was developed
with the help of the First Amendment Center and with religious
leaders' participation and buy-in, a great example for others. The
class doesn't just teach students about religious liberties and the importance of separating church from state. It teaches teachers and

school administrators how to handle religion in every aspect of the school day, giving educators the training that so many of them need.

Modesto has stood out because it has documented results focused on what a course on religion accomplished. Emile Lester, a political science professor at the University of Mary Washington in Fredericksburg, Virginia, and a research partner surveyed more than four hundred students in Modesto schools during the 2004–05 school year, four years after the program began. The researchers asked each student six multiple-choice questions about politics and world religions. The questions included choosing the name of the holiest city of Islam and figuring out which religion was founded by Siddhartha Gautama.[1] On the first pass, before taking the course, students got an average of 37 percent of the questions correct. In January, after the course, it was 66 percent. By May, students had lost ground; then, their average score was 52 percent correct. Lester, in his book based on the research, said his interviews showed that students were more likely to remember practical knowledge related to their daily surroundings than an array of facts. They won't forget how to recognize a Hindu *mandir*, he said, or forget why some Muslim women wear hijabs or Sikhs carry *kirpans*.[2]

Lester saw merits in the course but also thought teachers could take more risks. The course, he wrote, was fact laden. He reviewed the class materials and interviewed enough teachers to know that the school district's approach was to keep tight reins on the curriculum. The course emphasized religions' similarities more than their differences, while he believed religions should be defined by their differences, too. Taylor, the course's most ardent defender, said the way it was designed did not give teachers time to compare and contrast religions, and that was not their goal. They emphasize respect for all faiths and a basic understanding of various religions but avoid activities or lessons that would stack one religion against another. "The first commandment of teaching the course might as well have been, 'Thou shall not offend,'" Lester wrote.[3] Haynes, whose work helped shape the course, saw the Modesto class for what it was: "This is just the facts, ma'am." The city's schools were creating literacy about religions in the community. If he'd had a hand in creating the course, Haynes would have pushed for taking more risks.[4]

Lester's chats with teachers, like my conversations with them years later, showed that some resented being hamstrung. In the early years, they were not allowed to deviate from the provided binders of material or the approved videos for fear of offending someone. One teacher described the course guidelines as "districtspeak" created for the public's benefit and thought that many teachers would ignore the guidelines and still have thought-provoking conversations with students on religion.[5] McIntyre still avoided such discussions more than a decade after the course was created. Bucknam, my tour guide in the history museum and one of the course's first teachers, thinks many teachers were paranoid about causing controversy. He had no room to get creative because the course was so short and teachers were expected to cover so many religions. He did not buy the idea that teachers should not promote discussion with students, though he stopped short of allowing debate akin to what I saw in Wellesley when the sixth graders took on different sides in a discussion about a mosque expansion in Tennessee.

Niles Carlin, also one of the founding teachers, always tried to go deeper than the original course design and believed that high school freshmen could handle much more.[6] He wanted students to know that within each religion there was great diversity. After Carlin started teaching the course, he went back to college to earn a master's degree in Asian studies so he could speak with more authority about eastern religions. Carlin is a devout Christian who leads the chorus at the North Modesto Church of God, an evangelical church. He did not see his love for his faith being in conflict with his passion for teaching the course. If anything, learning about religions had grounded him more in his own beliefs. He could see the similarities and differences. He did not reveal his religion to his students until the end of the semester. He let them guess what religion he belonged to after the course's final exam. It delighted him to hear the variety of guesses. Some thought he was Buddhist. Others thought he was Jewish. Some would say Christian. To him, it proved he was teaching objectively.

He did not try to cram in instruction about ten religions. He focused on the big six and added some instruction about Confucianism and Daoism as a one- or two-day unit. He did not shy from letting students talk about their religion. Many Sikh students have shared their experiences, which he thought had made class more interesting. But he was careful to never out a student's religion and advised students to speak only for themselves, not for all Buddhists, or for all Christians, or for all Sikhs. He worked to reduce stereotypes not just of minority faiths but of Christians. He defined fundamentalists as true believers who were truly devout and noted that not all fundamentalism equals extremism. Given the reins, Carlin would turn the class into a one-year course and integrate religion even more into the lessons about geography.

Lester's survey results mostly painted a positive picture of Modesto's course. Nearly three-fourths of the students found it interesting or very interesting. After taking the course, more students were willing to stand up for the rights of religious minorities and defend a student whose religion had been insulted.[7] In the fall of 2013 I met with groups of students after classes at Johansen High School, where McIntyre taught. A handful of juniors, all of whom had taken the course already, said that at the minimum it taught them how to better deal with people from different cultures. They spoke to me in the hall outside of their Spanish teacher's classroom and they included an atheist, Catholics, and Baptists. One girl, who wanted to be a nurse and realized she would treat patients from different cultures and religions, talked about how she used to think women and girls wearing hijabs were weird. Now she understood better why they might cover their heads. She also predicted that, in the long run, she would know how to talk to someone from a different culture. Another girl thought just having the class was eye-opening because she had not known she could talk about religion at all in school. She did recall kids making fun of photos in the textbook, including pictures of Orthodox Jewish boys in ear locks that they wear because of a belief that the Bible forbids shaving or cutting hair in that area. Her teacher stopped the ridicule of the photos. A boy said his teacher, McIntyre, also stepped in when some students in his class taunted him for being an atheist. They had said, "Oh, you're going to hell." McIntyre interjected that the boy had the right to his own beliefs.[8] Modesto teachers were not naïve. They knew they could stop the teasing in the classroom if they caught it but that students could still act horribly once they entered the halls. Some kids will leave her class and still be bigoted and mean, McIntyre said to me as she ate lunch during one of her few breaks from classes. She wished there was a magic pill she could hand out.

But students who get the main message hear it strongly. One afternoon during lunch break I met with another group of teens, some just taking the course now and others veterans. We sat in chairs that students had pulled into the hall outside of McIntyre's classroom. Sierra Henry, a seventeen-year-old senior, was taking the class for the second time in the fall of 2013. She failed it as a freshman because she never turned in the required worksheet packets. She blamed having too many activities. A Protestant who attends a megachurch called The House, she said the class made her realize how little she knew about other religions. As a child, when she saw people with turbans she thought they were Hindus. She didn't know anything about Sikhs. She, like Alyssa Davis, grew up in a church where she was taught that her religion was the only right way. At first she thought she would get brainwashed in the class and worried about doubting her own religion. That never happened. She liked learning about other faiths and no longer thought people who followed them were weird or somehow inferior. She realized they were normal people with different beliefs.[9]

Sitting near Sierra was Janice Singh, a freshman who wore the uniform of youth in the area, close-fitting jeans with a creative mix of pastels, neon, and animal prints on her sweatshirt. Her thick black hair fell past her shoulders, covering some of the wires from the MP3 player headphones draped around her neck. Her outfit declared her determination to blend in, yet also her own unique style. Janice, a freshman who is Hindu, said she had long experienced prejudice and saw the ninth-grade course as a way for her to learn about other religions and, perhaps even more important, as a way for others to learn about hers. It is uneducated people who say stupid things about 9/11 to Hindus, she said. When Janice was in middle school a peer asked her if her father, an accountant at the Gallo winery, flew planes and whether he was a terrorist. Kids assumed that because Janice was dark-skinned and not black that she must be Muslim. She hoped the class would eliminate some of the ignorance and maybe whet students' appetites to learn more about Hinduism and other faiths. If they could learn more, perhaps the stares would stop when she happened to step out of her house in a sari.

Cynthia Rivera, a sixteen-year-old junior taking the class for the second time because she neglected to do the homework the first go-around, now sees the course as critical. While Cynthia is Catholic, her aunt converted to Islam when she married a Muslim man. The teenager has seen the way people treat the couple. She has heard kids at school make fun of Muslims and people practicing other minority religions and she doesn't hesitate to speak up: "I say, 'Why make fun of people?'" She credited the class with teaching her to step up for others. But she and other students, including those who took the course a decade ago, wished Modesto had taught them about different religions much earlier than high school. They wanted the school system to fill that gap.

Alyssa Davis and her younger brother, Steve, who also took the course from McIntyre, regretted that Modesto didn't start teaching about religion as early as elementary school. Alyssa wondered how schools could let children go on for so long in ignorance. She and her brother are haunted by a memory of a Sikh boy at their elementary school. Steve and his friends picked on the boy, who was perhaps seven or eight, and made fun of his turban. One of his friends pulled off the boy's turban. The boy was the only Sikh in class and they called him the Punjab. Alyssa tried to stop the teasing but could not. At the time, Steve had no idea what religion the boy was and presumed he might be a Hindu and believe in the elephant god. Sitting in McIntyre's class during the section on Sikhism as a high school freshman, Steve remembered the boy and felt stupid for not knowing he was a Sikh. He also felt bad that he had picked on the young Sikh boy but acknowledged a reality: kids do stupid things.

Steve was twenty-four, a month away from twenty-five, when I met with him at the same Starbucks where I had talked with his sister a few days before. He had just started at Modesto Junior College after serving in the Army for seven years, including fifteen months in Iraq and eight months in Afghanistan. The Modesto class altered his narrow worldview. He used to lump Hindus, Muslims, and Buddhists in the same place and figured, as his sister had, they were all going to hell because they did not believe in Jesus. The class changed his mind as he grew to understand that each religion taught about selflessness, sense of community, being courteous, and giving. In Afghanistan he met devout Muslims who gave him and his fellow soldiers food and tea when they met them on patrol. The class he had in high school gave him enough background that he felt comfortable asking Muslims questions about their religion. He learned from a Muslim in Afghanistan that the Koran also talks about Jesus and Mary, Moses, and even Noah. He learned that Jesus, like Mohammed, was considered a prophet to Muslims. If anything, Steve, like his sister, wished the course had taught him more. A human being, he said, should learn about other humans.[10]

Modesto has no plans to push instruction about religion earlier. Enochs, the superintendent when the course began and now long retired, said teachers could only do so much given the time they had with students. He thought society had romanticized children. Schools, he said, could not make little saints and tolerant people of all of their students because parents had them too much of the time and society bombarded children with too many various messages. What schools could do was soften some of the differences among children.[11]

But maybe it's at least worth trying to teach children about religion at an earlier age. Minneha, the magnet school in Wichita, isn't the only one giving lessons beginning in first grade. At a charter school in Malden, just outside of Boston, I watched as teachers taught their children the song "Go Down Moses" as part of the Core Knowledge first-grade lesson on the world's religions. The children learned that the song related to the story of Passover but also was a spiritual during the times of slavery in America. They seemed as excited about it as about any lesson they might receive.

In which grade should schools start teaching about religions? I'm not sure any age is too young if the lessons are delivered well and simply. During my son Simon's last year of preschool, as December arrived his teachers sent e-mails to all of the families. They asked us to tell them which holidays we celebrate, such as Christmas or Hanukkah, so they could incorporate each tradition into the classroom. They said they would talk about the various holidays in a fun, low-key way. So, if we brought something in, it should be a book or a game, and we should leave the more serious or religious traditions for home. I was a bit embarrassed to find out that I was the only parent who offered to do something. But Simon was thrilled and helped me plan what we would do about Hanukkah. He picked one book, *Mrs. Greenberg's Messy Hanukkah*, and I picked the other, *Chanukah Lights Everywhere*. We also made latkes in the kitchen together, though "together" might be stretching it. My son pushed the button on the food processor to grate the potatoes and the onions, and I did the rest.

The next day at my son's preschool, Simon sat in my lap as I read *Mrs. Greenberg's Messy Hanukkah*. The book says little about

Hanukkah and tells the story of an elderly woman babysitting a younger child who decides to make the potato pancakes and messes the kitchen. The children in the class sat on the floor in front of me and giggled as I read about how the kitchen kept getting messier and messier. Then I began reading Michael Rosen's book about the lights of Hanukkah and a boy's celebration with his family. I picked it because it seemed like it had a multifaith message. It wasn't just about the lights of Hanukkah. It was about how this was a season devoted to lights, and the Jewish family lit their candles on the menorah then walked around the neighborhood and admired the lights there for both Hanukkah and Christmas. Everything was going fine until I came toward the end of the book and read a line about how on the eighth night of Hanukkah, the young boy looked through a telescope at the stars and it was as if "God, too, were lighting his own menorah in the sky." My son, who had been sitting quietly, suddenly said, "God is the clouds." None of the other children commented, but I sat there not quite sure what to say. His teachers didn't say anything so I took my cue from them and just let the moment pass. It was an awkward moment because I knew there had to be many different views of God among the twenty children. I did not want it to seem like I was preaching anything. I was probably overreacting, but I wanted to heed the teachers' caution about not getting too serious about the religious part of the holiday. Hanukkah, in fact, was a minor Jewish holiday and one of the least religious. But the word "God" was religious. I followed up the books by showing the children a Noah's Ark menorah Simon had received as a Hanukkah present one year. Children asked questions like "How many candles do you light?" and "Do kids get presents?" They were curious about something they knew little about. At the end, I served latkes with applesauce.

Afterward, it nagged at me that I was the only parent who came in, even though the teachers were thankful. They had sent the e-mail because the majority of the children were already talking about Christmas and Santa Claus, and the teachers didn't want non-Christian children to feel left out. The teachers themselves did not do much direct instruction about the holidays or holiday activities with the children because they did not want to offend anyone. I wished, though, that someone had come in and talked about Christmas to the kids, or that the teachers had. They could have filled in a gap in my son's knowledge with a book that told even the basic story of Christmas. A friend of mine, whose son was in the class, said the teachers' note had immediately turned her off. As a devout Christian she did not know how she could come in and talk about her family's Christmas traditions without referring to the religious aspects. To her, it was not about the lights or Santa Claus. It was about Jesus.

My son's preschool, which was privately run, was on the third floor of a Baptist church, and when I took him home that December we always walked by the church's nativity scene. Simon would run up to it and look at the baby in the crib, the sheep, and the people gathered around the infant. I wondered for a moment whether I should attempt to explain what it all meant but decided against it. I was no expert on Christianity. I did not feel that comfortable talking about the meaning of Christmas with him nor did I know which storybook might work the best. I would have supported the idea of his teachers explaining Christmas to him as part of a bigger lesson about the holidays that different religions celebrate. It was almost ironic that the only lesson the kids received about the holidays was about Hanukkah. It was such a reversal from my own experiences in childhood.

When I began to crisscross the country, my son had just started kindergarten with children of several faiths, including Hinduism. His teacher didn't have a curriculum that incorporated world religions but did what teachers in the Lexington school system all were encouraged to do. At the start of the year, she asked parents, on a form, to share which customs, holidays, or traditions they marked at home. She used the answers to learn about her students' different cultures and throughout the school year read the children books about various holidays, including those celebrated by Christians, Hindus, and Jews. Following the school system's philosophy, she did not talk about one religion's holidays to the exclusion of others. For at least the past seven or eight years, all schools in my town have promoted the idea of teaching about the diversity of the students, whether that diversity stemmed from religion, ethnicity, or race. Teachers talk about customs, heritage, traditions, and family; religion naturally became a part of the conversation.[12]

Simon came home from school one day with a coloring page about Diwali, the Hindu festival of lights, and talked about hearing his teacher read a story about it. During the school's fall party, which fell around the time of both Diwali and Hanukkah, groups of children took turns doing activities with different parents. I paired up with another Jewish mother as we helped children decorate dreidels and told them a little about Hanukkah. A parent from India showed the kindergartners how to make holders for Diwali candles. Diwali came even more alive for Simon when Hindu neighbors delivered a box of chocolates, a Diwali tradition. Simon's kindergarten class, like his school at large, happened to be diverse, and the school's principal liked the focus on diversity rather than direct lessons about the world's religions. She did not think lessons on religion as a part of history were so critical in elementary school. I was not as sure.

When I listened to Debbie Fagg tell her first-grade class in Wichita about Jesus as part of a bigger lesson, I wished Simon were sitting there. She gave that lesson in a matter-of-fact way. In an ideal world, schools would do more in each grade level and give teachers the training they need to handle the subject with sensitivity and authority. They would, like Wellesley, go even deeper in sixth grade to try to at least eliminate religion as a bullying target in middle school. By high school, kids would know the basics and would be ready for even more material in world history and geography classes or in a required religion course like Modesto's. They would, like Modesto, train teachers and administrators on dos and don'ts about religion in schools. More teachers would become like the Modesto teachers who fought the promotion of one religion over another, even if simply meant pointing out that it was wrong to put "Merry Christmas" on the school marquee and ignore other religious holidays. Teachers and administrators, too, would learn that it was okay to allow students to run religious clubs on campus. Religion and public education do not have to be at odds.

Religion will always be a volatile subject. There is no escaping that fact. There likely cannot be a one-size-fits-all approach given the diversity across the nation, but maybe schools can do more than they do now. Sharon Peters had the best intentions when she asked students if they wanted to try on burkas and hijabs in the geography class she taught in the nearly all-Christian town of Lumberton, Texas. She knew students needed to know about the people beyond one little town's borders. More reports likely will be produced recommending ways to teach about religion, but the real power for making change lies with teachers. Teachers have the power to make sure religion takes its rightful position in education and that it never becomes the reason a child feels like she must slink away from her classroom.

I have had my own biases about evangelical Christianity because of my experiences as a child. During my recent travels, though, I met pastors from different evangelical churches and learned the same lesson that many teachers impart in world religion classes: not every person of a particular faith is the same. Yes, there are evangelical Christians who will tell me I'm going to hell because I don't believe in Jesus and try to convert me, but there are many others who don't act that way. Those of us in a minority religion constantly have to fight stereotypes and ignorance, as do atheists and agnostics, as do those in the religious majority. No one can evade it. An evangelical Christian pastor I met in my ultraliberal Boston suburb became so frustrated by the way others viewed his faith that he confronted the stereotypes on his business card with descriptors: "Evangelical, but not exclusive." "Biblical, but not doctrinaire." "Traditional, but not rigid."

I keep returning to the image that frightened Alyssa Davis in Modesto on that first day in her world religions class, an array of religious symbols on the classroom windowsill. Within a few weeks it became an image of beauty. She learned that belonging to one faith did not mean she had to shut others out. What if every school and every classroom could become that way, a place where all of the religions coexisted on the same shelf? And a place where students learned about all religions without fear, shame, or bias?

Acknowledgments

First and foremost, I thank Helene Atwan, my editor, for her wisdom and coaching and for her passion for *Faith Ed* from the beginning. Thank you as well to the entire Beacon team for support each step of the way toward publication. I can't name everyone, but special thanks to Susan Lumenello and Steven Horne for their care in copyediting and to Alyssa Hassan and Caitlin Meyer for their guidance on publicity and marketing.

Many people helped me make this book a reality. There were the numerous teachers, students, and educators who agreed to tell their stories after facing death threats and/or vitriol. There were those who not only shared their stories but opened up their homes to me for hospitality. Thank you, Yvonne and Ray Taylor, and Randy, Susan, and Sarah Benson. Author friends were also there for me in many ways. Susan Kushner Resnick acted as an extra set of eyes in the early stages, Jessica Keener and Carolyn Roy-Bornstein helped in the final stretch, and writing buddy Marjan Kamali was a booster from day one. Special thanks also to Francis Storrs, an assistant editor at the *Boston Globe Magazine*, for believing in this project from the start. GrubStreet, a Boston writers' organization, played a role, thanks to Joanne Wyckoff's book proposal writing class. Courtesy of decades in the newspaper business, my list of mentors is long, but this handful stands out: Carolyn Ryan, Sal Recchi, Paula LaRocque, Jim Memmott, and Mike Lafferty.

Tiferet, a literary journal, and *Moment* magazine gave some of this book an early home by honoring essays that became the basis for the chapter about my Ohio experiences. The Massachusetts Cultural Council, which gave me an award for an excerpt, also gave the book a boost well before publication.

This is a book about education and faith, and my temple community, my second family, and longtime friends have been supportive from day one. *Todah rabah* to all at Temple Isaiah of Lexington, especially Rabbi Howard Jaffe. Thanks, too, goes to my neighbor, Amantha Tsaros, and to my forever friend, Michele Boretti. My final words of gratitude go to those I love most: my family. Thanks, Mom and Dad, for all you've done to support my dreams and thank you to my in-laws, Maria and Norby, for helping out when I traveled on reporting trips. Thank you, Pavlik, for believing in this book, for believing in me, for being a wonderful reader, and for making it okay to leave the home front for weeks at a time. A final thank you goes to Simon, who has grown so much since I started this book. Nothing could make me prouder than to be your mom, but it sure made me smile to see how proud you were of me when you drew a cover of my book in a collage about the things you like at home. *Faith Ed* did indeed become a part of all of our lives.

Notes

PROLOGUE

1. Bedford schools superintendent Jon Sills described all of the incidents in a March 11, 2014, letter to parents and spoke about most of them at the March 12, 2014, forum at Temple Isaiah in Lexington, Massachusetts.

CHAPTER ONE *Burkagate*

1. Sharon Peters, in-person interview with author, September 20, 2013.
2. "A Short History of Hardin County Texas," compiled and written by Harold W. Willis, chairman, Hardin County Historical Commission, Kountze, Texas, 1998.
3. Steve Kellas, in-person interview with author, September 22, 2013.
4. Scott Mitchell, 1998 Lumberton High School graduate, in-person interview with author, September 27, 2013.
5. US Census data, 2010 Census.
6. US Census Bureau, State and County QuickFacts, 2008–12 estimate.
7. Texas Education Agency data on Lumberton Independent School District.
8. Gerald Chandler, Lumberton, Texas, schools' assistant superintendent, in-person interview with author, September 23, 2013.
9. US Census, 2010.
10. NBC News, "Texas Cheerleaders Can Keep Christian Banners, for Now, Judge Rules," October 18, 2012, http://www.nbcnews.com.
11. Associated Press, "Supreme Court Sets Aside Ruling Allowing Some Prayer in Alabama Schools," June 26, 2000.
12. Associated Press, "Supreme Court Lets Alabama Prayer Ruling Stand," June 19, 2001.

13. Lumberton parent Cindy Greene, in-person interview with author, September 25, 2013.

14. Mark Chancey, Southern Methodist University researcher of Texas Bible courses, telephone interview with author, January 17, 2013.

15. Terrence Stutz, "Texas Education Board Votes to Drop Evolution 'Weaknesses' from Curriculum," *Dallas Morning News*, January 22, 2009.

16. James C. McKinley Jr., "A Claim of Pro-Islam Bias in Textbooks," *New York Times*, September 22, 2010.

17. Tristan Hallman, "SBOE OKs Resolution Alleging Muslim Bias in Textbooks," *Texas Tribune*, September 24, 2010.

18. Class handout at Lumberton High School from online *NewsHour* curriculum. Lesson was excerpted from *Responding to Terrorism: Challenges for Democracy* (Providence: Brown University, Watson Institute for International Studies, August 2002).

19. John Griffing, "Students Made to Wear Burqas in Texas," *WorldNetDaily*, February 24, 2013, http://www.wnd.com.

20. Todd Starnes, "Students Told to Call 9–11 Hijackers 'Freedom Fighters,'" Fox News Radio, February 26, 2013, http://radio.foxnews.com/toddstarnes/top-stories/students-told-to-call-9-11-hijackers-freedom-fighters.html.

21. Lumberton Independent School District response to CSCOPE and Promotion of Islam statement, February 25, 2013.

22. Editorial staff, "Lumberton Burqa Incident Needs Clarity from School Officials," *Beaumont (TX) Enterprise*, March 1, 2013.

23. E-mails to school district officials, provided through Freedom of Information Act request.

24. Lumberton schools superintendent John Valastro, in-person interview with author, September 26, 2013.

25. E-mail to Sharon Peters, anonymous sender, February 2013.

26. Peters interview.

27. Poster of notes by Sharon Peters's students.

28. Clarissa Pinkola Estés, *Women Who Run With the Wolves: Myths and Stories of the Wild Woman Archetype* (New York: Ballantine, 1996), inside cover text.

29. Board meeting material is from audio of the meeting and subsequent interviews with those in attendance to confirm attendance figures.

30. Student who wore the burka in Facebook photo and mother, in-person interview with author, September 22, 2013.

31. King James Bible, John 16:2–4.

32. US Religious Knowledge Survey, 2010, Pew Research Center's Religion & Public Life Project.

33. Valastro interview.

34. Background on See You at the Pole, *See You at the Pole* website, http://syatp
.com.
35. Muslim family, in-person interview, September 27, 2013.
36. Peters, telephone interview with author, October 6, 2014.

CHAPTER TWO   *Did a Field Trip Put Students in the Lion's Den?*
1. Peter Schworm, "Mosque Says Students Weren't Pressed to Pray," *Boston Globe*,
September 18, 2010.
2. Reader comments at end of *Wellesley Townsman* online article, September 17,
2010, http://wellesley.wickedlocal.com/.
3. Adam Blumer, in-person interview with author, March 17, 2011.
4. Tour of Islamic Society of Boston Cultural Center mosque with guide, July 26,
2011.
5. News release from the Islamic Society of Boston Cultural Center, September
17, 2010.
6. Based on my 2011 visit to the mosque and interviews with the tour guide.
7. Mosque news release.
8. Author's 2011 mosque visit and telephone interviews with mosque officials
about makeup of worshippers.
9. Americans for Peace and Tolerance video, "Wellesley Students Learn to
Pray to Allah," posted on YouTube, https://www.youtube.com/watch?v=Z7
-I9Qp3d4Y.
10. Jackson Posnik, in-person interview with author, June 27, 2011.
11. Ibid.
12. Calli Posnik, in-person interview with author, June 11, 2011
13. Edward Schumacher-Matos, "Bowing to Hysteria Over a Field Trip," *Washington Post*, September 25, 2010.
14. Draft of Rabbi Joel Sisenwine's sermon, September 2010.
15. Bella Wong, in-person interview with author, October 29, 2010.
16. Linda K. Wertheimer, "Test of Faith," *Boston Globe Magazine*, August 28, 2011.
17. Ibid.
18. US Census Bureau, 2010 Census.
19. Pastor Martin Copenhaver, in-person interview with author, July 2, 2013.
20. US Census Bureau, 2010 Census.
21. Pew Research Center Religion & Public Life Project, summary of key findings
of US Religious Landscape Survey, 2008, http://religions.pewforum.org
/reports.
22. Bella Wong, telephone interview with author, August 2013.
23. Blumer, telephone and in-person interviews with author, March 2011 to spring
2013.

24. Annual letter from Blumer to Wellesley Middle School parents.

25. Visit to Wellesley Middle School, April 6, 2011.

26. Jonathan Rabinowitz, in-person interview with author, August 22, 2013.

27. Celia Golod and parents, in-person interview with author, June 2, 2011.

28. Zain Tirmizi, in-person interview with author at school, May 2011.

29. Ali Zain and Hadia Tirmizi, in-person interviews with author, May 2011 and August 2013.

30. Important Sites: The Prophet's Mosque, part of University of Wisconsin-Madison and Wisconsin Public Radio website, "Inside Islam: Dialogues and Debates," http://insideislam.wisc.edu/.

31. Roxbury mosque tour guide, telephone interview with author, October 15, 2013.

32. Wertheimer, "Test of Faith."

33. Celia and Lisa Golod, in-person interviews with author, June 24, 2013.

34. Wellesley high school students, in-person interviews with author, July 11, 2013.

CHAPTER THREE *Whose Truth Should They Hear?*

1. Account of Chuck E. Cheese's story is based on in-person interviews with Steinbrenner High School students, Hassan Shibly, and teachers in Tampa, Florida, February 24–27, 2014.

2. Dan Herbeck, "Muslim-Americans Held at Border Lose Suit," *Buffalo News*, December 23, 2005.

3. Jill Gregorie, "Living with War," *Generation*, University of Buffalo student publication, 2006 issue.

4. Unsigned editorial, "Speaker Controversy a Complicated Issue," *Clarence Bee* (NY), April 14, 2010.

5. Hassan Shibly, in-person interview with author, February 25, 2014.

6. Copies of the original and updated Clarence school board policies and e-mail exchanges with school board president Michael Lex.

7. Hassan Shibly, "Clarifying Remarks I Made Years Ago Regarding Hezbollah," June 28, 2011, http://www.hassanshibly.com/.

8. Kelly King, Steinbrenner High School principal, in-person interview with author, February 25, 2014.

9. Kelly Miliziano, in-person interview with author, February 24, 2014.

10. Father who made original complaint to Steinbrenner, in-person interview with author, February 26, 2014.

11. Southern Law Poverty Center Intelligence Files, profile of Pamela Geller, http://www.splcenter.org/get-informed/intelligence-files/profiles/pamela-geller.

12. Pam Geller, "Child Abuse: Hamas-Linked CAIR Poisoning Minds of High School Students," *Atlas Shrugs* blog, December 4, 2011. www.pamelageller.com.

13. Account of phone calls among the father who complained, Kelly King, and Kelly Miliziano are based on in-person interviews with author in February 2014.

14. Quotation from Pastor Martin Niemöller, on poster in Steinbrenner High classroom. Numerous versions of his quote/poem exist, according to US Holocaust Memorial Museum website.

15. Interview with father who made original complaint.

16. Pamela Geller, "Hamas High School in Florida," *American Thinker*, December 19, 2011, http://www.americanthinker.com/articles/2011/12/hamas_high _school_in_florida.html.

17. Miliziano interview.

18. Neil MacFarquhar, "Muslim Groups Oppose a List of 'Co-Conspirators,'" *New York Times*, August 16, 2007, and previous articles about the foundation's court case.

19. Pamela Geller, "Hamas-Linked CAIR in Your Kids' Classroom: A Parent's First-Hand Account," *Atlas Shrugs* blog, January 5, 2012, http://pamelageller .com/2012/01/hamas-linked-cair-in-your-kids-classroom-a-parents-first-hand -account.html/.

20. Kelly Miliziano, recollection of threatening phone call, telephone interview with author, January 2014.

21. Terry Kemple, in-person interview with author, February 24, 2014.

22. Daniel Ruth, "Terry Kemple's School Board Candidacy a Columnist's Conundrum," *Tampa Bay Times*, April 20, 2013.

23. Articles on CNN and in *USA Today*, and other publications, August 2012. Kemple recommended David Barton as an expert on America's founding as a Christian nation. Barton's book, *The Jefferson Lies*, was withdrawn by its Christian publisher in August 2012 because of the book's inaccuracy.

24. All school board meeting comments come from webcasts of the meetings, available at the Hillsborough County School Board website, http://sdhcweb casts.com/index.html.

25. E-mails to Kelly Miliziano in the aftermath of guest-speaker controversy.

26. All speaker comments are from school district video of February 28, 2012, Hillsborough County School Board meeting, http://schoolboard.hcpswebcasts .com/.

27. Laila Abdelaziz, telephone interview with author, March 31, 2014.

28. CNN video of President Obama's Town Hall meeting in Tampa, Florida, January 28, 2010.

29. Hassan Shibly, in-person interview with author, February 26, 2014.

30. Guidelines handed out to Hillsborough County School Board at board meeting of February 28, 2012.

31. Shelli Barton, in-person interview with author, February 27, 2014.

32. Daniel Krasnove, letter to the editor, *Tampa Tribune*, January 27, 2012.

33. Laura Gonzalez, in-person interviews with author on two occasions, February 2014.

34. Austin Ransdell's testimony to the board and board member comments come from audio of the meeting.

35. David Caton, "Tampa Could Be One of America's First Sharia Compliant Cities," post on Florida Family Association website, n.d., http://www.florida family.org.

36. Miliziano interview.

37. Charles C. Haynes, author, and Natilee Dunning, editor, *A Teacher's Guide to Religion in the Public Schools* (Nashville, TN: First Amendment Center, 2008), 4.

38. Marlene Sokol, "Anti-Muslim Group, Protestors Face Off," *Tampa Bay Times*, September 12, 2012.

39. Kelly Miliziano, telephone interview with author, January 14, 2014.

40. Kelly King, telephone interview with author, March 4, 2014.

41. Al Nafea, in-person interview with author, February 27, 2014.

42. Hepah Hussein, in-person interview with author, February 27, 2014.

43. Joan Wadler, telephone interview with author, March 10, 2014.

CHAPTER FOUR   *How Young Is Too Young?*

1. Numerous Associated Press and *Washington Post* articles on evolution and gay marriage battles in Kansas.

2. Background on Summer of Mercy and George Tiller murder from *New York Times*, *Wichita Eagle*, and Associated Press.

3. Kristina Gaylord, "Dockum Drug Store Sit-In," entry on Kansas Historical Society website, June 2011, http://www.kshs.org.

4. Fred Mann and Stan Finger, "Mosque That Burned Had Received Anti-Islam Letters, Leader Says," *Wichita Eagle*, October 31, 2011.

5. Mahmoud Al-Hihi, principal of Annoor Islamic School, in-person interview with author, November 12, 2013.

6. Lisa Hansel, communications director, Core Knowledge Foundation, telephone interview with author, fall 2013.

7. E. D. Hirsch Jr., ed., *What Your First-Grader Needs to Know: Fundamentals of a First-Grade Education* (New York: Dell, 1997), 111–34. Revised edition by the Core Knowledge Foundation. Material used is from history and geography introduction.

8. Core Knowledge Foundation provided materials on grade-level curriculum.

9. Patricia Watson Hunt, executive director of elementary schools, Oklahoma City Public Schools, telephone interview with author, April 10, 2014.

10. Diane Ravitch, on *Diane Ravitch's Blog*, August 23, 2013, www.dianeravitch.net.

11. Mary Schumacher, Minneha principal, 1998–2003, in-person interview with author, November 15, 2013.

12. Schumacher interview.

13. Richard Whitmire, "Core Knowledge Boosts Scores, Tough Curriculum Yields Elementary Gains in Oklahoma," *USA Today*, May 30, 2000.

14. Deborah Fagg and first-grade teaching colleagues at Minneha Core Knowledge Elementary School, in-person interviews with author, November 12, 2013.

15. Ibid.

16. Kyle Ecklund, in-person interview with author, November 11, 2013.

17. Ecklund interview.

18. Family Letter, Core Knowledge Foundation.

19. Linda Bevilacqua, president of Core Knowledge Foundation, telephone interview with author, October 17, 2013.

20. Liz, Larry, and Benjamin Karp, in-person interview with author, November 12, 2013. All subsequent quotes and information from the Karps came from this interview and from an earlier phone interview.

21. Account of Karps' view of bulletin board display comes from interview at their home, November 12, 2013.

22. Liz Karp interview with author, November 12, 2013.

23. *Bare Naked Islam* website posting, August 19, 2013, http://www.barenakedislam .com.

24. Sampling of hate e-mails sent to Minneha administrators and Wichita school officials, August 2013.

25. Charles C. Haynes, "By Removing Islam Display, Kansas School Surrenders to Ignorance," First Amendment Center religion commentary, August 22, 2013.

26. Wendi Turner, Dana Sachs, and other fourth-grade teachers, in-person interviews with author, November 12, 2013.

27. Travis Perry, "Kansas Lawmaker 'Appalled' by Islamic Display in School," Kansas Watchdog.org, August 19, 2013, http://watchdog.org/category/kansas/.

28. Salsabila, Suad, and Kamal Attaria, in-person interviews with author, November 13, 2013.

29. John Allison, superintendent of Wichita, Kansas, school system, in-person interview with author, November 14, 2013.

30. Angelique Badgett, second-grade teacher, in-person and phone interviews with author, November 2013.

CHAPTER FIVE *The Church Lady*

1. Recollection of meeting with Van Buren superintendent based on past interviews with my parents.

2. Golda Meir, *My Life* (New York: Dell, 1976), 1.

3. *The Lord Is Not on Trial Here Today*, 2011 documentary by Jay Rosenstein.
4. James McCollum, foreword to Dannel McCollum, *The Lord Was Not on Trial: The Inside Story of the Supreme Court's Precedent-Setting McCollum Ruling* (Silver Spring, MD: Americans for Religions Liberty, 2008).
5. Plaintiffs' motion for summary judgment, Lawrence A. F. Ford, et al., Plaintiffs, v. Dr. C. W. Manuel, Defendants, US District Court, Northern District of Ohio, Western Division.
6. Background on *Ford v. Manuel*, the suit against Findlay schools, comes from August 8, 1985, opinion and order, 629 F. Supp. 771, U.S. District Court, N.D. Ohio, and articles in the *Courier*, Findlay, OH.
7. Ruthann Walters, in-person interview with author, March 11, 2013.
8. Material about reaction to Ford case stems from author's conversations with editors at the *Courier*, March 11, 2013, and author's telephone interview with Marc Young-Williams, Ford's attorney, June 6, 2014.
9. Dorothy Powell, in-person interview with author, March 12, 2013.
10. "The Hancock County Religious Education Story," February 2, 2010, one-page document, provided to the author by Dorothy Powell.
11. Interpretation based on author's April 18, 2013, telephone interview with Charles C. Haynes as well as many books on the country's church/state history.
12. 343 U.S. 306, Zorach v. Clauson.
13. I would have loved to have used the beautiful lyrics of "The Butterfly Song," but the publisher declined permission, saying it allows use only if it believes the lyrics will be used in the spirit in which they were written.
14. Dorothy Powell, phone conversation with author, April 7, 2013.
15. Shirley Winch, in-person interview with author, March 11, 2013.
16. 533 U.S. 98 (2001), Good News Club et al. v. Milford Central School.
17. Michael Brand, in-person interview with author, March 2013.
18. Charles C. Haynes, *A Teacher's Guide to Religion in the Public Schools* (Nashville, TN: First Amendment Center, 2008).
19. Van Buren High School student, in-person interview with author, March 13, 2013.
20. Rosemary Salisbury, in-person interview with author, March 13, 2013.
21. Dwight Groce, social studies consultant at Ohio Department of Education, telephone interview with author, June 6, 2014.
22. Pair of Van Buren high school students, in-person interviews with author, March 13, 2013.
23. Stephen Prothero, *Religious Literacy: What Every American Needs to Know—and Doesn't* (New York: HarperOne, 2007).
24. Jack Marshall and Jennifer Obenour, telephone interviews with author, January 16, 2014.

25. Jim Heath, "New Law Allows School Credit for Religious Studies," WBNS-10TV, Columbus, OH, June 13, 2014, http://www.10TV.com.

CHAPTER SIX *Carefully Taught*

1. Alyssa Davis, in-person interview with author, October 1, 2013.

2. Several Modesto teachers, in-person interviews with author, September 29 to October 3, 2013.

3. James Enochs, in-person interview with author, October 1, 2013.

4. Robert Michaelsen, *Piety in the Public School* (New York: MacMillan, 1970), 238.

5. *The Function of the Public Schools in Dealing with Religion*, report on the exploratory study by the Committee on Religion and Education (Washington, DC: American Council on Education, 1953), 7.

6. Abington School District v. Schempp, 374 U.S. 203 (1963).

7. Jay D. Wexler, "Preparing for the Clothed Public Square: Teaching About Religion, Civic Education, and the Constitution," *William and Mary Law Review* 43, no. 3, article 6 (2002).

8. Michaelsen, *Piety in the Public School*, 246.

9. Nicholas Piediscalzi, foreword to "Past, Present and Future Directions in Public Education Religion Studies," in *Civility, Religious Pluralism, and Education*, ed. Vincent F. Biondo III and Andrew Fiala (New York: Routledge, 2014).

10. Nicholas Piediscalzi, telephone interview with author, July 16, 2013.

11. Piediscalzi, foreword, 18. Note: Piediscalzi lists source for the Clark quote as "Personal Reflections on the Schempp Decision," in *Religion Studies in the Curriculum: Retrospect and Prospect, 1963–1983*, ed. Peter Bracher et al. (Dayton, OH: Public Education Religion Studies Center, Wright State University, 1974.)

12. Piediscalzi interview.

13. James C. Carper and Thomas C. Hunt, *The Praeger Handbook of Religion and Education in the United States, Volume 2: M–Z* (Westport, CT: Praeger, 2009), 322.

14. James C. Carper and Thomas C. Hunt, *The Praeger Handbook of Religion and Education in the United States, Volume 1: A–L* (Westport, CT: Praeger, 2009), 30.

15. Ibid., 31.

16. Various sources, including Charles C. Haynes and Diane Moore, a Harvard Divinity School professor.

17. Michael Waggoner, editor of *Religion & Education* journal and history of education professor at University of Northern Iowa, telephone interview with author, July 22, 2013.

18. John Seigenthaler, foreword to *Finding Common Ground: A First Amendment Guide to Religion and Public Schools* (Nashville, TN: First Amendment Center, 2007).

19. Waggoner interview.

20. Charles C. Haynes, in-person interview with author, June 19, 2013.

21. Ibid. Haynes's recounting of what he said in Modesto in that meeting in 1990s.

22. US Census, 1970.

23. US Census, 2000 and 2010.

24. Tour of McHenry Museum, October 2, 2013, and material from Bob Santos and Lisa Bruk, eds., *Stanislaus County History: An Anthology* (Modesto, CA: Press and Publications Board, McHenry Museum & Historical Society, 2004).

25. Yvonne Taylor, in-person interview with author, September 29, 2013.

26. Amanda Pazornik, "ADL Offers Reward in Modesto Synagogue Vandalism," April 2, 2009, http://www.jweekly.com.

27. Emile Lester, *Teaching About Religions: A Democratic Approach for Public Schools* (Ann Arbor: University of Michigan Press, 2011), 1.

28. Membership numbers from the temple website, www.modestogurdwara.org/ (accessed July 31, 2014).

29. Associated Press, "Autopsy Shows No Sign of Foul Play in Death of Sikh Man," September 19, 2001.

30. Description of Sikhism based on author's interviews with Sikhs as well as the essay "Key Features of the Sikh Faith," by Bajinder Pal Singh, published April 19, 2012, using Amazon Digital Services.

31. Gurbax Kaur Singh, principal of Sikh Temple of Modesto's religious school, in-person interview with author, September 29, 2013.

32. Bhupinder, Ruby, and Jaspal Padda, in-person interviews with author, October 1, 2013.

33. History of the world religions course comes from in-person and telephone interviews with several sources, including founding teachers, Jennie Sweeney, Haynes, and retired superintendent James Enochs, and from a written history of the course's development by Yvonne Taylor.

34. Rules for the teachers come from the document "Guidelines for Teaching World Religions" that is used in Modesto.

35. Nathan Schar, Johansen High School principal, in-person interview with author, October 2013.

36. Information on Jessica Ahlquist comes from multiple articles and a talk the author attended in April 2013.

37. Sherry McIntyre, in-person interview with author, October 1, 2013.

38. From a PowerPoint slide and history of Williamsburg Charter, outlined in *Finding Common Ground: A Guide to Religious Liberty in Public Schools*, written and edited by Charles C. Haynes and Oliver Thomas (Washington, DC: First Amendment Center, 2001).

39. McIntyre interview.

CHAPTER SEVEN *Raising Religiously Literate Americans*

1. World Religions course survey questions, provided by Emile Lester.
2. Emile Lester, *Teaching About Religions: A Democratic Approach for Public Schools* (Ann Arbor: University of Michigan Press, 2011), 125.
3. Ibid., 136.
4. Haynes interview, June 2013.
5. Lester, *Teaching About Religions*, 136.
6. Niles Carlin, in-person interview with author, October 3, 2013.
7. Lester, *Teaching About Religions*, 119.
8. Johansen High School students, in-person interviews with author, October 1, 2013.
9. Sierra Henry, in-person interview with author, October 3, 2013.
10. Steve Davis, in-person interview with author, October 2, 2013.
11. Jim Enochs, former Modesto superintendent, in-person interview with author, October 2, 2013.
12. Sandra Trach, principal of Estabrook School, Lexington, MA, telephone interview with author, July 21, 2014.

INDEX

FAITH ED.